The Admissions Essay

THE ADMISSIONS ESSAY

How to Stop Worrying and Start Writing!

by Helen W. Power, Ph.D.
and Robert DiAntonio, Ph.D.

A Lyle Stuart Book
Published by Carol Publishing Group

Carol Publishing Group Edition, 1995

A Lyle Stuart Book
Published by Carol Publishing Group
Lyle Stuart is a registered trademark of Carol Communications, Inc.

Editorial Offices: 600 Madison Avenue, New York, NY 10022
Sales & Distribution Offices: 120 Enterprise Avenue, Secaucus, NJ 07094
In Canada: Canadian Manda Group, One Atlantic Avenue, Suite 105
Toronto, Ontario, M6K3E7

Queries regarding rights and permissions should be addressed to:
Carol Publishing Group, 600 Madison Avenue, New York, NY 10022

Manufactured in the United States of America
ISBN 0-8184-0436-1

15 14 13 12 11 10 9 8 7 6 5 4

Carol Publishing Group books are available at special discounts
for bulk purchases, sales promotions, fund raising, or
educational purposes. Special editions can also be created to
specifications. For details contact: Special Sales Department,
Carol Publishing Group, 120 Enterprise Ave., Secaucus, NJ 07094

Library of Congress Cataloging-in-Publication Data

Power, Helen W.
      The admission essay
        1. College applications—United States. 2. Exposition
(Rhetoric) 3. Essays. I. DiAntonio, Robert. II. Title.
LB2351.52.U6P69   1987   808'.066378   87-10170

ACKNOWLEDGMENTS

The authors wish to thank the many college admissions officers and high school college counselors and senior English teachers who have generously offered their help in the preparation of this book. Our particular gratitude goes to Robert Hendrin, director of admissions, Washington University; Charles Beech, director of admissions, Webster University; Harold Wingood, associate director of admissions, Duke University; Carmel Calsyn, Crossroads School; Rabbi David Eisenman, Block Yeshiva High School; Dwight Hatcher, Peggy Tracy, and Nancy Barton, Clayton High School; Karen Massie, University City High School; Eloise Mayer, Metro High School, St. Louis Public Schools; Sister Helen Santa Maria, Nerinx Hall High School; James Shapleigh, Webster Groves High School; and Bonnie Vega, St. Louis University High School.

We are particularly grateful to students who let us see their application essays, and to students in composition and writing classes at Washington University and Webster University whose experiences in essay writing have helped us understand the problems and the process.

Our thanks go to Joan DiAntonio for typing much of the manuscript, to Richard Power, and to our children, Aaron DiAntonio and Carla Power, model application essay writers of the past, and Adam DiAntonio and Nick Power, model application essay writers of the future.

PREFACE

No task in the entire admission process causes students as much anxiety as does the writing of the application essay. Applicants know that a poor essay can weaken the effect of strong GPAs, SATs, or class rank. On the other hand, a good essay can strengthen the application that might suffer from a less-than-dazzling academic record.

This book is designed to help applicants write successful essays. It can be used by the student on his or her own or in a classroom or college counseling setting.

The Admissions Essay is divided into two parts.

In the first part, Chapters I and II outline the role of the application essay. Chapters III and IV provide a step-by-step guide to writing it. Chapter V cites common problems students face—and shows how to solve them; Chapter VI offers remedies for the common mistakes admissions officers find in essays.

The second part of the book includes more than 50 actual application essays written by students who were admitted to distinguished colleges and universities. This section includes questions that an admissions officer might ask when reading the essays, and comments on most of them.

These essays have worked. They are not model essays—if such exist—but rather show how various students have approached the problem of the essay. For anyone interested in young people, these essays provide a view of an age and of a time, and of young people looking at themselves and the future.

Both the "how-to-do-it" section and the sample essays are offered in the hope that they will help student applicants find their own voices in their own essays and that their essays will help them find the future they want.

CONTENTS

ESSAYS THAT RESPOND TO SPECIFIC QUESTIONS

Contents

I

THE APPLICATION ESSAY: HOW IT CAN HELP YOU—OR HURT YOU

GPA 2.8; Class standing: 55/300; SAT 530V/560M; ACT 19; AP History 3; Captain, basketball team; secretary, senior class; 22 credits; Projected major: business

Thousands of printouts like this one reach admissions officers at colleges throughout the country. More significantly, thousands reach single colleges with only hundreds of places. Prep schools, private and parochial schools, and junior colleges receive similar data sheets, as do graduate programs and professional schools. Scholarship, honors and award programs get their share.

These printouts reveal statistics and other facts. They don't reveal *the person applying*. The country music fan, the science-fiction buff, the party animal, and the D&D devotee all hide behind the same statistics. The quiet, the lively, the whimsical, the comic, all look alike.

Each applicant is more than a sum of scores, or even

the sum of the best recommendations from teachers and alumni. The admissions application essay helps give the school a picture of the applicant. Hundreds of colleges ask each applicant to write as many as four personal essays. Candidates for special programs and scholarships must often write even more.

How Do Admissions Committees Use the Essays?

Essays help the committee select and reject applicants.

• Highly competitive colleges (for example, Ivy League schools, Stanford, Carleton, Pomona, Rice) receive many more applications from exceptionally qualified students than they have places in the freshman class. (Recently, Harvard drew more than 13,000 applications for approximately 2,100 places.) Admissions officers use the essays to help distinguish one able student from another.

• Even schools which accept a larger percentage of their applicants still turn to the essay for help deciding who's in, who's out. The essay is especially important for students whose GPAs, class rank, or test scores are near the bottom of the accepted group.

• Graduate and professional programs (including some law schools and MBA programs) traditionally relied on interviews and academic records. Recently, they have turned to the essay to help identify the best of the large pool of qualified applicants.

• Boarding prep schools and small colleges are especially concerned about their campus community. Essays reveal the character of potential community members.

• Some schools—Williams College, for example—reserve places for students who would not ordinarily be admitted but who have special talents, talents often revealed in the essay.

• Most schools seek a diverse student body and a variety of interesting people. The essay identifies the water skier, the magician, the future farmer; the rest of the application does not. An applicant may not have a good academic record; he or she may not have been active in sports or school activities. But if he or she spent the summer spelunking or organizing a program for under-privileged pre-schoolers, the admissions committee reader may sit up and take notice.

• Schools with special characteristics (a school that emphasizes a religious or social commitment, or one that has extensive independent study programs) will use the essay to identify applicants they want.

• Some prep schools and colleges pride themselves on spotting diamonds in the rough—students with poor records, but great potential. Those students' essays are often the clue the committee needs.

How Much Weight Does the Committee Give the Essay?

Some schools weigh the essay very heavily. The application for St. John's College is, in effect, a series of essays; Bowdoin and others indicate the essay's value by not asking for SAT or ACT scores. Other schools put the importance of the essays further down the list—after class standing, or grades, or test scores.

But any school that asks for an essay from its applicants can and may give it considerable weight.

Harold Wingood, associate director of admissions at Duke, says, "A strong candidate can effectively destroy his chance if he does not handle the essay carefully and truthfully."

On the other hand, a candidate whose scores are not strong may gain admission through the essay. Charles Beech, director of admissions from Webster University, notes that applicants from highly competitive high schools often have relatively low class standing but are potentially excellent college students. The essay gives the committee a better feel for the student's academic performance, particularly in English.

A truly stunning essay can compensate for many statistical lapses.

No applicant who wants admission can safely neglect the essay. The only possible exception: the student whose scores and grades are so near the top of the usual range for the school to which he is applying that admission seems assured. But even that applicant risks the committee's ire. And this applicant is offering a poor vision of himself, a vision that may return to haunt him for four years.

The application essay is not only a kind of traffic signal: Stop/Go; In/Out; Accepted/Rejected. The essay introduces you. It helps the school get to know you even before you arrive on campus. And it stays with you.

• Prospective freshmen at some small colleges are amazed to receive letters of acceptance from directors of admission that allude specifically to their essays. "I chuckled when I read about your windswept tent in Maine," said one letter of acceptance. "You might be interested in our campus Outdoors Club or 'Y' when you enroll." This prospective freshman's essay was read—and noted.

• One Yale freshman was awed when a famous scholar was designated his adviser. He was overwhelmed when she greeted him at an orientation week dinner with questions about politics in the third world country in which he'd lived. She'd read his application essay.

• Other applicants have received mail from faculty members about their essays—even before they were admitted. One young woman wrote about composing the score for her high school musical. She got a warm, friendly letter from the head of the college's music department. The essay alerted the school to her particular talents.

Your essay does not disappear after you're recruited, admitted, and welcomed. Most schools hang on to it. *Your essay stays with your records,* lodged—depending on the school—with your dean or with your adviser, who usually reads it before he or she meets you. The application essay is part of the permanent record. It doesn't go away.

• Many schools use the essay as an aid to academic counseling, particularly for non-traditional students—that is, students who have returned to school after considerable absence or who have changed the direction of their education.

• Larger schools keep records of students' special talents, which are often revealed in the essay. If the theater department needs an expert juggler or if the campus lecture committee wants someone who had been active in S.A.D.D. to meet a guest speaker, they consult the records.

Ideally, the admissions essay serves as a kind of marriage broker—or a well-worded personal ad in a singles classified paper. It brings the mutually suited—in this case, the student and the school—together. *The essay not only helps the admissions committee: it helps you present your case for admission.* By the time you apply, much of your application is predetermined: you've taken your tests, gotten your grades, chosen your activities. You present the *results* in your application. But your essay is still to be written. *The essay is the major part of the application that is still under your control.*

The college application is probably the first time you will be judged and valued primarily on the basis of written records. And it may be the first and only time someone has asked you to describe yourself, explain yourself, evaluate yourself. And will read what you write.

The essay allows you to:

Present yourself as you are
("People think I'm an intellectual lightweight, but I'd rather be writing poetry than watching 'Cheers'");

Show your personality
("When I set out to do something, nothing will stop me");

Add information not requested elsewhere in the application
("The quality I most prize in myself is loyalty to friends");

Explain other parts of your application that may not appear favorable
("There are several reasons why I failed chemistry");

Show how your mind works
  ("Baby sitting for twins is a lot like cheerleading");
Show your intellectual interests
  ("When I picked up my first Ray Bradbury novel, I knew why I had learned to read");
Reveal your knowledge about the school to which you are applying
  ("I want to spend four years with people willing to take the responsibility for operating an honor system.")

In other words, the essay allows you to explain yourself.

The process of writing the essay should help you learn about yourself—which is, after all, what education is primarily about.

Along with the stories we hear about pain and suffering involved in writing the essays, we got encouraging stories from students who had learned about themselves—and from parents, allowed to read the essays, who had learned about themselves, too.

One potential drama major said, "I never really knew why acting was so important to me until I had to explain it on my application."

A divorced mother, who read her son's account of that difficult time in the family's life: "I cried for days when I read it. But I understood for the first time what that experience had been like for Nick."

The process of writing the essay pays off—in self-knowledge, in understanding, in expanded feelings of self-worth—long before the letters of acceptance arrive. In a sense, taking the writing of the application essay seriously is the best preparation for being a freshman.

II
WHAT DOES THE ADMISSIONS COMMITTEE *REALLY* WANT?

Every applicant's dream or nightmare is that some word or phrase or concept will make the admission committee reader grin with pleasure and acceptance—or frown with disapproval and rejection.

You worry: Should I tell them I'm a Republican? Left-handed? A rock drummer? Should I write something funny or something serious? *What is going to work?*

Admissions committees discuss the *types* of candidates they want to admit and the *profile* they would like for the freshman class. Often committees discuss (and argue and disagree about) sample essays: Are the essays good? Should the writers be admitted? Some schools share such deliberation with alumni, particularly alumni who interview prospective students, and with high school counselors and English teachers. Other admissions officers say frankly, "We don't know what we want. But we know it when we see it."

However, admissions committees have no secret agenda. No special button that the writer can hit that will guarantee admission or rejection. No passwords. No magic phrases. They do not meet under cover of darkness to evolve strange and obscure rules to defeat uninformed candidates.

In fact, most committee members try to keep from being fickle. Or picky. Or prejudiced. Or unfair. They try to be open to a candidate's strengths, not probing for his weaknesses. (Perhaps the exception is competitive schools inundated with qualified applicants. Readers here are as eager to find reasons not to admit excellent candidates as reasons to admit them.) Admittedly, sometimes a candidate will be unlucky: the reader may be tired or annoyed. Almost all schools, though, guard against arbitrariness by having several readers of an application. At other times, candidates can be lucky: at one Eastern school, an admissions committee member spotted a candidate with a background strikingly similar to his own— Quaker, rural, midwestern—and took an interest in the applicant, and the student after he was admitted. Some schools allow admissions committee members one or two "free" choices: they can admit a candidate who would not otherwise be admitted, but who is particularly appealing or interesting to them. Generally, candidates get a fair shake, with little left to the whims or prejudices of individual readers.

Admissions committees may not have hidden messages. But they do send clear messages to applicants. Unfortunately, not all applicants read the messages. You need to be able to figure out what the readers want. There are two main ways:

1. Pay attention to the messages the school sends to you through its catalogues, recruiters, and alumni interviewers. These messages tell you the school's self-

described character.

2. Read carefully the message from the admissions committee about what it wants. The committee tells you what it wants in its requests for essays on the application. (As you plan your essay, return to the instructions on the form. This helps avoid the hazard of being unwittingly blown off course.)

Committees' requests for essays can be categorized in three groups:
The general autobiographical essay.
The focused autobiographical essay.
The essay on a specific topic.
The most commonly requested essay is the *general autobiographical essay*. Here's how some schools request it:
"Tell us about yourself."
"Give the admissions committee information about yourself that is not included elsewhere on the application."
Some schools request a *focused autobiographical essay* instead of or in addition to the general essay. The requests look like this:
"What word best describes you?"
"Give us page 400 of your 500 page autobiography."
"How would you like to be remembered?"
"What is the most significant thing about you?"
"Choose one extra-curricular activity and describe its importance in your life."
Some schools ask candidates to write *essays on specific topics*, topics that are not ostensibly autobiographical. Here are some requests for such essays:
"If you could create a public holiday, what holiday would you create?"

"Who is the person who has most influenced you?"
"If you could spend one evening with a famous person, with whom would you spend it?"
"What is your favorite book?"
"What is your favorite art work?"
"What invention does the world most need?"

Some schools use the same questions every year; other schools change questions.

The Common Application, which is accepted by approximately 100 schools, asks for a personal statement on one of three topics:

1. Evaluate a significant experience or achievement that has special meaning to you.
2. Discuss some issue of personal, local, or national concern and its important to you.
3. Indicate a person who has had a significant influence on you, and describe the influence.

These questions allow the writer to discuss his or her own life (experiences or achievement or a personal concern) or topics external to him or her (another person, a public concern). The questions provide some focus, but not a particularly narrow one. In each discussion, the writer is asked to include his or her own personal relation to the topic.

What Do the Readers Expect from the Responses to These Essay Topics?

• All essay topics are designed to give the committee a sense of you as a person.
• All essay topics are designed to give the committee

some idea of how your mind works.

Schools want to admit real people, not computer print-outs. You need to give them the sense of the person applying.

Most importantly, you need to present yourself, not someone else. If you don't read the *Odyssey* every night before bed, don't claim you do. You will be found out. Or perhaps worse, your essay will not ring true: it will sound fake and tinny. Besides, though every school is seeking a variety of students, the person you create might not be the person the school is looking for.

Present yourself in all your individuality and complexity. Don't blur your self-portrait so that you look like everyone else. In fact, *most admissions officers and college counselors advocate risk-taking*. What do they mean?

They mean risking to show yourself as *you really are*.

They mean risking to take an offbeat or unusual subject *that really interests you*.

They mean risking to argue *a position in which you really believe*.

They do not mean sensationalism for the sake of being sensational, or eccentricity merely to catch the reader's eye. Rather, they admire the courage of a writer who sincerely presents his or her own originality.

As an applicant, you want to present your best self. No use asking admissions officers to love you at your worst. Your friends and parents may. But will Tulane? Rice? Or the University of Virginia?

What follows in this book will help you present your best self to the admissions committee. It will help you write an essay that is true to yourself and is helpful in gaining you admission.

How to Present Yourself in the Three Basic Types of Essays

THE GENERAL AUTOBIOGRAPHICAL ESSAY

This essay can give the reader the landmarks of your life, the landmarks you choose to point out. You can include thoughts, events, experiences, honors, defeats, people and places that comprise your life. You can tell the reader whether you are rich or poor, shy or bold, orphaned, a Girl Scout, a traveler, an acrobat, a computer whiz. These aspects of your life give the reader a feeling for you as a person.

However, the essay should give the reader something more valuable than the external circumstances of your life: *your reaction to your experiences.* The reader is moderately interested in whether an applicant has worked at Burger King (that gives reality to the application; it may show initiative or diligence or willingness to work or interest in money or need for money) or has been to Europe (that may show exposure to other cultures). But the admissions committee reader is much more interested in your interpretation of your experience: your analysis of it; your response to it; your valuation of it. Did you like your job or trip? What did you learn from it? What disappointed you? Were you changed by it?

The general autobiographical essay should record your thoughts and feelings about the selected substance of your life.

THE FOCUSED AUTOBIOGRAPHICAL ESSAY

The focused autobiographical essay has the same aims as the general one. In it you should stress interpretation and analysis of your life, not merely record your life. It's easier to write in one important way: the readers have narrowed the topic for you, given you a smaller field to plough. Your toughest job may be fitting what you want to say into the narrowed topic.

THE ESSAY ON A SPECIFIC TOPIC

Like the two other kinds of essays, the essay on a specific topic introduces you to your readers. But this type of essay emphasizes you as a thinker. The readers are less interested in autobiographical details than in what you think, feel, and value. In writing this essay, your first job is to pick a subject. But the choice of the substance of your answer is less important than your reasons for your choice. That is, you won't be admitted because you choose Aristotle and not John McEnroe for a dinner guest, nor will literary criticism of *Peter Rabbit* insure rejection, *Portrait of the Artist as a Young Man* acceptance. The more obviously intellectual choice may show something, but your explanation of your choice shows something more substantial.

The topics for essays suggest what the readers want you to write. But sometimes admissions committees leave the form as well as the content open.

• Several schools (Tulane, for example), ask applicants to do anything they want with a blank sheet of paper or a rectangular space. Results are various: schools report interesting verbal responses that are not essays (e.g., verse epics; short plays) and non-verbal responses (collages, drawings, graphs, formulae, a musical score.)

If you have a choice of topic or form, which question to choose?

The one that feels most comfortable to you; the one that stimulates or interests you most; the one that you can answer most meaningfully. The committee is offering you a genuine choice. No question is better than another.

One caution: Ask yourself if your option best reflects both your own strengths and the qualities of the program to which you are applying. For example, if you are applying for a pre-med program, you might choose to write an essay rather than draw a picture. On the other hand, a score and not an essay might be appropriate if you expect to enter a music program.

If the school leaves the choice to you, take advantage of the options. But if the type of response is prescribed, or the topic choices limited, take heed.

The Most Successful Essays

Almost every admissions person, high school counselor or student adviser we spoke with spontaneously recalled his or her favorite essay. They spoke enthusiastically of essays that had captured their attention, support—and their recollections. The characteristics of these essays:

• Honesty. The student writer addressed the subject without pretense or false sensationalism. The essays weren't phony.

• Thoughtfulness. The writer avoided clichés—or thought through clichés so that they were presented newly minted. The essays avoided superficial observations and pat solutions.

• Sensitivity. The writer revealed his or her values. Even when the subject of the essay was the writer's own life, he or she showed awareness of the rest of the world.

• Liveliness. The essay revealed a writer actively engaged with his or her subject, making the reader engaged with the essay.

Perhaps surprisingly these favorite essays were not often about highly intellectual subjects or about extraordinary experiences. Most were about ordinary experiences (so ordinary many writers avoid them), but ordinary experiences freshly and carefully examined.

. Writers of the successful essays took risks. The risks were not often in the writer's taking a bizarre topic or making a sensational presentation. The risk involved avoiding well-worn paths of thought and presentation. The risk involved daring to be honest and to think through the issues. The risk involved revealing the writer as he or she is—not as the writer thought the reader would want him or her to be.

III
GETTING STARTED

You have read the requests for essays.

If you are offered a choice, choose. If you can't choose, go through each option with the strategies described below.

If you are writing a general autobiographical essay or a focused autobiographical essay, you must select subject matter. You can't describe your whole life—even in a multi-volume autobiography, even if you are no older than 17.

Some applicants answer the general autobiographical essay question with a *chronological account* of their life, not with an essay that has a subject or central controlling idea. In effect, they ask the reader to take a ride in time with them, and they point out the landmarks as they go by.

• When the writer has interesting comments to make on this chronological ride, the approach succeeds.

• When the writer has a controlling theme or attitude or a controlling theme that he or she sees working in the life, such an approach succeeds.

• But usually, this approach *does not succeed.* The essay tends to bog down in detail ("And then we moved to Muncie"), and it tends to lack insights into the writer's life. The reader may end up with the facts of the applicant's life, but not the spirit.

Usually, then, you need a subject for the essay. The best subject finds you: it grabs you by the shoulder and insists that it be written about. This happens when you are interested in the subject. *Your genuine interest in the subject is the single most significant ingredient in a successful essay.*

You can make yourself aware of your interests. You can make your topic find you. How? Brainstorming. An easy way is to follow one or all of the following three basic strategies:

> Think about yourself as a person.
> Think about your experience.
> Think about one school to which you are applying.

Engage in one or all of the strategies well before you actually write your essay. Brainstorm on paper. Or talk to someone. Or think through the issues on your own. Your preparation for writing is an important part of the process.

Strategy I: Thinking About Yourself

If a college asks you to "tell us about yourself," you probably automatically think about what you are like and how you appear to others. You are following Strategy I: Thinking about Yourself.

How best to engage in this strategy? Following are several techniques:

1. Start a list of adjectives or of qualities and traits that describe you. Ask your friends or family for help. Are you

intelligent?	curious?
sports-minded?	loyal?
friendly?	argumentative?
energetic?	sentimental?
sociable?	ambitious?
competitive?	hard-headed?
laid back?	

Make your adjectives as specific and as concrete as possible. "Intelligent" is good, but "quizzical," "analytical," "well-informed," "curious," "thoughtful," are more precise and more telling.

• Select one to three main qualities you think important.

• Find an event or experience in your life in which these qualities are best shown. Write about it.

Carmel Calsyn, college counselor and English teacher at Crossroads School, a private school in St. Louis, has her seniors fold a sheet of paper in half. On one side they write qualities they like about themselves; on the other side, they list incidents or events that substantiate them.

2. Think about your future—ten years or so down the road.

What would you like to be doing? What kind of person would you like to be then?

What is the relation between the person you are now and the person you want to be?

How are you going to become what you want?

Use your vision of yourself in the future as a key to analysis of yourself.

3. Think about your past. Are you different now from what you were a year ago? Two years ago? Have you changed your goals? Your values? Your interests? Your personality? Why? When? How? Your change (your growth, your development) makes a good topic for an autobiographical essay.

Some applicants focus best not on themselves and their own character and personality, but upon the experiences that have helped create their character and personality.

Strategy II: Thinking About Your Experiences

In this strategy, think about your experiences, using the journalist's questions "Who?" "What?" "When?" "Where?" to help you answer "Why?" The answers to these questions will help you write about yourself.

Start brainstorming with a list of "Who?" questions:

Who most influenced me?

Whom do I most admire?

Whom would I like most to be like? (If it's not the person I most admire, why the difference?)

Who was the first person who really made me think?

Who made me look at myself in a new way?

Who gave me some information or knowledge or skill or emotional support that really helped me?

What do I want to be doing in 5/10/20/30 years?

What event seems most significant in my life?

in the life of my country?

in recent times?
What is my favorite pastime? Book? Movie? TV
show?
When did I decide I wanted to go to college? Prep
school?
When did I first feel responsible? Independent?
Where have I lived?
Where do I want to live?
Where would I most like to visit?
Where is the power center in the U.S.?
As you have probably noticed, some of these questions
sound like the specific questions particular schools suggest
on their application. Answering them should give you a
subject.
• Note questions that take you a long time to answer.
That could suggest that you have lots to say about them.
• Note groups of questions that might provide groups
of interesting answers.
The answers suggest something about you. If the person you most admire is Desmond Tutu or Nancy Reagan,
that should give you a clue to the kind of person you are.
If your favorite pastime is lying in a hammock, your essay
may be different from that of a person who says his favorite pastime is windsurfing.
Remember: the experience or subject alone will not
suffice. Even the most arresting experience is one you
share with many students. For example, many applicants
are AFS students or Boy Scouts, admire Winnie Mandela,
enjoy David Letterman. The subject matter is not
unique: you need to interpret and explain your experience.
Another caution: Don't rush to record your participa-

tion in a particular program, without first examining your experience. Boy Scouts, AFS, Model UN are designed to provide particular experiences. For example, a rock climbing program may have been designed to give participants the feeling of independence and self-confidence. Dwight Hatcher, Clayton (Mo.) High School college counselor and former admissions officer at Kenyon College, calls these experiences "created experiences." Whenever possible, students should choose to write about "creative experiences" rather than ones created for them, he suggests.

He notes that an essay that merely records that the program succeeded in its aims tells the admissions committee little about the applicant.

Strategy III: Thinking About the School to Which You Are Applying

When you started looking at schools, you thought about the schools' special qualities. Think about those special qualities when you write your autobiographical essay.

Does the character of the school to which you are applying lead you to want to talk about some part of your personal life?

For example, a small residential prep school or college might be especially concerned about the applicants' ability to fit into a small community. A large urban university might look for independence in a candidate. A school with a strong moral or ethical bent might respond to an applicant's similar concerns. A school that allows students freedom in developing their own programs will seek independent students who have already made some decisions about their interests.

The school's special qualities might prompt a topic for an autobiographical essay. If you are applying to a business school or a vocational program, examine your entrepreneurial experiences. For a creative arts program, consider experiences you've had in dance or in the graphic arts.

Don't, however, change your life story to fit the image of the school or college.

Do use the image of the school to prompt analysis.

Use this strategy as a double check on your plans. If you are applying to business school and keep wanting to write about the joys of a potter's wheel, think twice about a business major. If you find yourself impatient with the niceties and fine distinctions of an honor system, ask yourself whether you should attend a school that emphasizes one.

The Specific Questions: Strategies for Responding to Them

The strategies for finding answers to specific questions are similar to those for finding a subject for autobiographical essays. You need to spend time thinking—brainstorming—to come up with an answer that can be developed into a fruitful essay. The essay depends first on coming up with an answer—a name of someone most influential, of a book most admired.

If you need to write about a person (most influential, most interesting, most memorable, or most admired), think of two categories: people you know personally, and people you know because they are famous.

For people you know personally, think of

family.
friends and their families.
teachers and coaches.
neighbors.
employers and fellow workers.
When you think of people who are famous, think of
people in various fields:
sports.
entertainment.
politics and government.
religion.
Think of people who lived long ago (recall your history
classes and your Sunday School lessons) and of people
who live today (glance through *Time* or *Newsweek*, the
daily paper).
For books, your pattern of brainstorming will seem less
obvious. Here are some tricks to refresh your memory:
1. Consider frequency: Which books have you read
more than once?
2. Think about conversations with friends. Do you
allude to any characters? That is, do you talk about people you have read about? Do you refer to incidents from
the stories? For example, do you say that the president of
the community service club is just like Holden Caulfield?
Or that the Halloween party recalls *Lord of the Flies?*
Remarks such as those would suggest that you have not
only read *Catcher in the Rye* or William Golding's novel,
but have incorporated it into your life.
3. Look at lists; browse. Your school library has reading lists; your school has course reading lists.
Once you have thought of a person or book that seems
important to you, you can proceed to think of the actual
significance to you in terms of the topic. The name, the

title, will get you started. They will unlock your memory. Allow yourself time to think about the subject of the specific question. At first, you need not set aside particular time. But make yourself focus on the subject when you are doing something else—brushing your teeth, walking to school. Soon after you have a thought that *may* be useful, jot it down. No harm—even if you don't use it. If you don't jot it down, you may never think of it again. Think of yourself as an archeologist collecting fragments to recreate an ancient building. You may pick up more fragments than fit, but you want to guard against throwing anything away prematurely.

These strategies for developing content for your essay suggest one of the most important rules in essay writing: *Don't try to write the application essay at the last minute.*

You need time.

Time to choose the question.

Time to think of the subject.

Time to decide what you want to say.

You need all that time *even before* you start to write.

IV
GETTING IT ON PAPER

You've already done the hard part: the thinking. If you have done sufficient thinking selecting the subject, the actual act of getting your tale on paper should be easy. *The first draft of the essay should almost write itself.*

Get it down on paper fast. Don't worry about quality. Don't fuss over word choice, organization, effective opening paragraphs. Deal with those issues later, in the subsequent drafts necessary for a good product.

When it comes to putting your thoughts in shape, you will be calling upon all your training—formal and informal—in essay writing. Your writing has been developed and tested not only in English classes, but in letters home from camp and in notes slipped into lockers and in Model UN proposals and club reports and minutes. Much of this training is so much a part of you that you are not conscious of it; some of the training you may want consciously to call back to you for the occasion of writing the application essay. You may want to look over some texts you've used in English class about writing essays or you might want to talk with teachers who have helped

40

your writing. You probably will want to do this *after* you have first draft—your initial ideas—on paper.

Texts and teachers will provide good advice on writing essays in general. *Following are special suggestions for application essays.*

Two rules:
1. Check your essay for unity, organization, and coherence.
2. Be able to state the central idea or thesis of your essay in a single, complete sentence.

How to check your essay for unity, organization, coherence:

• *Unity.* Each essay should have a single topic. You may be able to write an essay about winning the state free throw tournament and suffering through your parent's divorce *if those two experiences are related.* If they are not— even if they are both major events in your life—choose only one.

How to determine whether the topics are really connected? Ask yourself how you plan to go from one subject to another.

If you find yourself saying, "And another thing . . ." or "A second important event . . ." or "Something else that has affected me . . ." you have two subjects, not one. Choose one.

On the other hand, if you find yourself thinking, "The strength I gained in living in a family experiencing a divorce helped me face the State Tournament," or "I worried about my parents' divorce on the way to State," your subjects are connected. They can both appear in the same essay. (Common ways that subjects are connected and so may be treated as unified are through cause/effect;

through sharing common qualities; through being examples of a more general subject; through occurrence at the same time or in the same place.)

• *Organization.* Your essay will come to your mind in a particular order—often chronologically, that is, the way things happen in time. Ask yourself if chronological organization is best. After all, you have choices. Consider alternative orderings.

REVERSE CHRONOLOGY. Instead of talking about preparations for a bike trip, the trip itself, and the subsequent evaluation, consider opening your essay with the return from the trip. Often retrospect works best.

CAUSE/EFFECT. "The trip was destined to be a failure for several reasons. Let me tell you first the reasons, then what the trip was like."

EFFECT/CAUSE. "I am the first member of my family to call myself a Republican. Strangely enough, my political awakening occurred at the dining room table."

GENERALIZATIONS FOLLOWED BY EXAMPLES OR REASONS. "My high school is a training ground for Yuppies. Following are the reasons."

"All my life, I have chosen friends who are on the fringes of society. Here are descriptions of some of my friends."

SPATIAL RELATIONS. "My room reveals me. If you look at the walls, you will see . . ."

COMPARISON/CONTRAST. "I thought France would be an open liberal society, but I found it more closed and narrow than that of my Iowa town."

"Playing football is similar to and different from playing basketball."

Weigh the merits of surprising the reader at the ending of your essay against the merits of indicating the results or important idea first, then guiding the reader through the issues that led up to the results. In other words, choose whether you want an inductive or deductive pattern. There is no single correct organization. The material itself should suggest the best way of ordering, as should your awareness of your reader's needs. Thinking about the organization will help you think more clearly about your subject.

• *Coherence.* Do parts of the essay stick together? Do parts seem related to one another? Choosing a single topic will help achieve coherence, as will finding an appropriate organization. But you still need transitional words or phrases or sentences or repetition of words or of sentence patterns. These help the reader move from one idea to another and to see connections. For example:

"The second reason [or "another reason" or "the most important reason"] I was glad I transferred to Country Day. . ."

"The first day was bad. The rest of the week was terrible."

"I was proud I won the contest. However, that was not the most important part of the experience for me."

State the Central Idea or Thesis of Your Essay in a Single Sentence

This sentence need not appear in your final essay, though it is usually a welcome beacon to your reader. Even if you don't use the sentence, framing it will encourage you to unify and focus your essay and will guarantee that your essay says something. A good thesis sentence should make you feel good about your essay. A bad thesis sentence is a sign that you may need to improve your essay.

Here are some bad thesis statements:

"This essay is about my parents' divorce." (What about it? The sentence does not reveal the direction of the essay.)

"There are good things and bad things about being a twin."

"There are many reasons that Central is a good high school."

(These sentences are empty. You need to identify and limit the reasons. You also need to think whether an essay that ends up balancing perfectly the good with the bad will be a forceful one.)

Here are some thesis statements that may be all right—but probably won't be:

"Being named prom queen was the most exciting event in my life." (This sentence implies that the essay is going to be a description of how exciting the prom is, which is self-evident. Does the writer really want to describe the evening? Is she really saying anything new?")

"I became involved in the anti-apartheid movement because apartheid is terrible." (Few would disagree. The committee is interested in you or your view of the political situation, not the political situation.)

"Socrates is a great man." (Agreed. So what else is new?)

Here are some good thesis statements—suggested revisions of the preceding bad ones:

"My parents' divorce eventually helped me to mature, but first it made me behave like a little kid."

"Being a twin helped me to realize who I really am, but it also made me realize I'd never be the person I wanted to be."

"Central High School has good classes and activities, but wonderful faculty and students."

"As a self-professed intellectual, I learned something about myself and my real values the night I was named prom queen."

"I realized all the privileges I have after I became active in the anti-apartheid movement at school."

"I think Socrates was a great man because he shared his wisdom with others."

Everything just said about the essay in terms of unity, organization, and coherence, and about the importance of a good thesis statement, can be said about the paragraph. The paragraph is an essay writ small. Your thesis statement becomes a topic sentence; you have decisions to make about singleness of topic, organizational patterns, and coherence.

These rules for getting your story down on paper are also tests as to whether your essay is readable and understandable. They promote clarity, and they help your reader understand what you are saying.

Adjusting Your Essay to the Reader

To review:

You've figured out what the admissions committee is asking for.

You've looked at your life and found a subject.

You've thought about your subject over a period of time. You've unified and organized your essay and made sure that it hangs together. What more can you do? You can make certain that the essay sounds like you, that the *voice* in the essay reveals you as you really are. And you can make certain that the voice in the essay speaks in an appropriate way to your *audience*.

Every essay has a voice in it, the voice of the writer as he or she is, or chooses to be, or mistakenly presents himself or herself. This voice reveals the attitude towards the subject and toward the audience.

Often you have thought about "psyching out the teacher"—finding out what he or she really wants. And you've probably been ashamed to think that, because it seems slightly manipulative and fraudulent.

Yet ancient Greek and Roman philosophers did not think "psyching out" the reader or listener fraudulent. When they developed the art of rhetoric they recognized the need for an essay or speech to be adjusted to its audience. Lawyers take into account the predilections of judges who will read their briefs. Lawyers and rhetoricians recognize that the most logical and truthful of arguments do not necessarily convince unless they suit the listener or reader. Awareness of your audience will help the audience understand you.

Different people need to hear different things from us depending on what they know and what they're interested in. And we behave differently—and write differently—when different people are involved. For example, a letter declaring affection or respect is different if it goes to your parents, your girl or boy friend, your kid brother, or a teacher or clergyman.

Identify your audience. What can you assume about the readers of your application essay?

• The audience is varied. Don't assume the whole committee is a clone of the single interviewer or campus representative you met. Committee members vary in age and experience, and in tolerance for and interest in your essays. But you do know some things.

• Your readers will be reasonably intelligent and well educated. (*US News and World Report* quotes a Harvard interviewer, however, saying, "We make a career out of rejecting people who are brighter than us.") The intelligence and education of the committee members means something in terms of audience. *Don't talk down to your reader.*

This is a losing statement:

"Let me explain to you the true meaning of a liberal education since most people don't understand it."

Recast the same idea into a sentence sensitive to your readers' qualifications.

"Though definitions for a true liberal education vary, some are clearly wrong. As I see it, a true liberal education should be . . ."

• The audience has authority over you: your reader will determine your acceptance or rejection at a certain school. Under the misapprehension of being assertive, don't be disrespectful—a smart aleck, a cheeky upstart. But under the misapprehension of being polite, don't be sycophantic either: don't suck up to the readers. Losing statements:

"Only a short-sighted school would refuse someone with my qualifications."

On the other hand, the readers won't believe this:

"It would be the greatest honor of my life if people

so distinguished as the Admissions Committee of Podunk College chose me to become one of the members of the illustrious school community."

Instead, recast the same ideas, cutting the excesses:

"I think I am qualified to be a student at your school."

"I would be honored to be admitted to Podunk College."

• The audience has or should have a realistic attitude toward its school. Part of your audience's job is to root for its own school, to be a loyal supporter. But assume that the audience is neither stupid nor naïve.

Don't be condescending toward the school:

"When I messed up on my SATs and realized I couldn't get into Northwestern, I also realized I could get a good education at your school."

"I hope to be admitted to Podunk since I am better than most of your students. My SATs and GPA are above the scores you list."

On the other hand, don't be falsely flattering:

"Everyone should realize that Podunk gives a much better education than Cal Tech or Oxford."

• Your audience is older than most of you, but it may include recent graduates as well as veteran admissions officers. However, these readers are fairly familiar with the main landmarks of the adolescent landscape. You need not explain the story of *Catcher in the Rye;* the title and author will suffice. However, your audience probably doesn't know your local scene: you may need to identify "Old Beady Eyes." On the other hand, a name like "Hamburger Home" is probably self-evident or explained by context.

• Your audience is probably comfortable in the fields of

humanities or social sciences, but less comfortable in technical, obscure or highly specialized fields. That is, your reader can follow a discussion of *Catch 22* even if he or she hasn't read it or an analysis of the social scene on the Upper East Side even if he or she has never left Texas. But an essay that outlines a chemistry experiment or expounds on a fine point of Talmudic interpretation will probably lose your reader. Such subjects are best understood in human, personal terms:

What I learned from the experiment.

How the experiment helped me understand myself.

Why I was excited about the interpretation of the Talmudic passage.

• Assume your audience is sympathetic to you, but don't depend on audience sympathy to get you an indulgent reading.

If you assume that your audience is your antagonist, your tone will be hostile, irritating, belligerent. If you see your reader as your enemy, you will turn yourself into an enemy of the reader.

Note the antagonistic tone of these statements; note the suggested revisions:

"Elitist schools like yours often do not understand the values in the lives of workers."

Instead:

"My experience in the working class may seem strange to Ivy Leaguers."

Or:

"You probably don't think that knitting is a suitable occupation for a boy since you probably have the same false stereotypes as most of society."

Instead:

"Many people are surprised that a boy knits."

• On the other hand, don't assume that your audience is so sympathetic that you need not persuade it of your excellence. Your audience is not your mother. When you hear yourself thinking, "Oh, they'll understand," "They know what I mean," you know that you are relying too heavily on the support of your audience. Clearly stated ideas, fully developed ideas, correct spelling and grammar, will mean that the audience will be able to develop sympathy toward you.

• Remember your audience's particular interests. Remind yourself of the school's character. Essays for a school with a religious emphasis, with a specialized program (vocational, liberal arts, etc.), with special features (a major work/study program, a large international program), might be sensitive to the particular interests of the audience.

When you think about your readers and your subject, you will be able to decide what language to use. Remember: you are telling someone about your life and your feelings. *Use relatively informal, edited English.* That is, use the language of conversation, not the language of a sermon or the Internal Revenue Code. But make certain that your language has been cleaned and polished. Grammatical mistakes, careless word choice, do not mean informality; they mean sloppiness.

Resist the efforts of well-meaning adults to alter your style to sound distant, formal, objective, and cold. Many older people were trained to write when the pronoun "I" and contractions were frowned upon. Writers wrote of "one's" relationship with "one's family" and did not, could not, and would not—instead of didn't, couldn't, and wouldn't—use contractions. Such rules are appropriate for some kinds of writing. They are not appropriate for an admissions essay, which functions to convey the feeling of you as a person. Read your essay aloud to yourself. Does it sound like you? If not, perhaps you are too formal.

Your prose is like a mirror that catches and reflects you. It often reveals what you don't expect—sometimes what you don't want. Do you say what you mean to say? Listen to your tone of voice in your essay. Decide whether it reveals you as you really are.

One Southern high school senior writes, "I will soon be graduated from this so-called institution of learning." (She suggests here that she doesn't think her school is much of a school. Perhaps that's going to be one of the points of the essay. If it isn't, does this bit of sarcasm belong? Does she want to reveal herself as sarcastic for no purpose?)

Another candidate writes:

"My brother also likes to write stories, but he don't master the fine points as me." Here, the ungrammatical presentation suggests that he has not mastered the art, as he claims he has. What the writer says is at odds with the way he says it.

Such a discrepancy between what applicants say and what they reveal is found often in essays that feign enthusiasm. Essays that praise education or claim that an AFS experience was wonderful or that a job is valuable often reveal themselves to be hollow.

• Readers aren't convinced when essays involve only clichés or platitudes—familiar statements that are not fresh or new.

• Readers aren't convinced when essays are not particular or specific, but are vague and general.

• Readers aren't convinced when the generalizations ("My French host family was wonderful and friendly") and the details run in opposite directions (tales of pantries

off limits, silent evenings, exclusion from family gatherings).
Make certain the tone of voice reveals you.
Make certain that your reader does not receive incompatible messages from your essay.

Getting the Essay Ready to Send Off

The essential ingredient of the successful essay is time.
Time to think.
And re-think.
Time to write.
And re-write.
Time to read. And re-read. And to proofread. And to proofread again.

Your essay is your product. Write it yourself. Type it yourself. If a school asks for the essay in your own handwriting, comply.

Many admissions people caution against asking your mother's secretary to type up your final essay on the latest office equipment. The professional-looking product suggests you may have received professional help in writing. Don't make your readers suspicious.

Proofread it yourself. Re-read it yourself. An interested friend can help you by reading and proofing your final essay along with you. But yours is the final responsibility.

The finished essay will reflect you. And your ideas. It will address any audience. It will help you get admitted to school. And it will stay with you.

V
THE APPLICANTS' VIEW: COMMON PROBLEMS—AND HOW TO SOLVE THEM

Every year, a new group of applicants suffers over writing the application essay. The reasons are not new. Most of the writers have common problems, a common core of woes.

For common problems, we offer solutions.

If you're having trouble writing your essay, see if your problem—and its solution—follows. Identifying your problem puts you on the road to solving it.

Do you hear your own complaint in those of fellow students?

Common Problem #1: "Nothing Interesting Has Ever Happened to Me"

Like everyone else, people who read college admissions essays like exciting tales and exotic stories. But admissions officers know their job is to select a freshman class. They can read tales of adventure in their spare time. On the job, they want to read essays in which applicants, responding to application requests, talk about themselves.

Readers value a thoughtful, original approach to everyday experience more than they value an insensitive, stereotypical approach to an unusual one. Applicants who rely too heavily on the whiz-bang experience can find that it blows up in their faces.

If your life has included a sensational experience that is significant to you, by all means write about it. But don't rely on the unexamined experience to get you in the door, no matter how impressive the experience is. Schools *do not* admit candidates merely because they were lucky enough to go to Europe, meet a bear at Yellowstone, or dine with Mayor Koch. Nor do they grant entrance automatically to those who have survived earthquakes, parents' divorces, or tents blown over on camping trips.

Such experiences make good subjects—if the writer is perceptive, analytical, and thoughtful. But everyday, ordinary experiences viewed by the intelligent student will make better essays than sensational events recorded thoughtlessly.

Look at the sample essays at the end of this book. Note how many successful essays view familiar experiences (working at McDonald's, running in a track meet, receiving emotional support from a parent) with freshness and liveliness.

Common Problem #2:   "I Can't Find a Subject"

"I know what I want to write about, but I can't get started."

If you can't find a subject, don't panic. Look at Chapter III for ways of brainstorming. Allow yourself more time for thinking. Most of the work of writing does not involve actually writing, but the thinking that precedes it.

If you have found a subject, but can't get started writing, don't try to start at the beginning of the essay. Many professional writers write the opening paragraph last. They have to find out what they're actually going to say before they can introduce the essay to a reader.

To get started writing:

First, jot down whatever comes into your head that is associated with the subject:

    words

    phrases

    ideas

    sentences and paragraphs.

Next, write down bits and pieces of the essay. Don't try to order your work.

Third, come back to your work the next day. And the next.

Fragments of thought, once written down, have a way of expanding and arranging themselves under your continuing surveillance.

Common Problem #3: "I Can't Tell Them What My Favorite Book Is. They'd Think I was Stupid"

"I haven't read anything worth writing about." "An intellectual experience? They've got to be kidding."

Many applicants are paralyzed with guilt because they haven't *read* and *relished* Churchill's complete diaries or

The Origin of Species every night before going to bed. They fear their actual experiences and tastes will not impress the admissions committee. These applicants make major mistakes.

1. They grit their teeth, write an essay on a book they're "supposed to like." They can say little about the book—because they have little to say. *If you have read a book but have no interest in it, don't write about it.*

2. Embarrassed by their choice of the real book that influenced them, they write scanty, undeveloped essays. These writers are afraid to focus on their "embarrassing" choice. You should remember:

   a. As with every other issue related to the essay, it is not the subject you pick, but what you say about it, that counts.

   b. Admissions committees do not expect you to be a completely formed intellectual. You wouldn't need college if you were.

   c. Libraries are full of autobiographies by intelligent, important people who find major inspiration in trivia. You are not stupid if you suddenly understand uncle/nephew relations by seeing Dewey, Huey, and Louey, and Donald Duck, rather than Hamlet and Claudius. *Be honest.*

   d. Magazines and newspaper reviewers discuss books of a wide range of quality, and do so with varying skill. It is just as possible to discuss Nancy Drew mysteries intelligently as it is to discuss Jean-Paul Sartre stupidly.

But no one would argue that Nancy Drew mysteries are as good (as serious, as profound, as valuable, as subtle) as Shakespeare. How do you deal with the reality of your taste and your desire to appear thoughtful and intelligent?

Explain why the book you choose is your favorite or why it influenced you most.

• Don't say merely that it is interesting (that's circular; no one likes something that is boring); don't say merely that it is exciting (so is a roller coaster ride) or "realistic."

Tell instead why it is interesting:

Does it tell you something you didn't know?

Explain something you didn't understand?

Talk about people like those you know or different from those you know?

Tell why you found it exciting—and why you like exciting reading.

What unexpected turns did the plot take?

Tell why you found it "realistic."

Do characters behave like those you know?

Are the situations familiar?

Following are some comments from good essays on favorite or influential books. Notice how the writers have made thoughtful, perceptive comments.

"The Hardy boys stories may seem childish, but those books gave me my first ideas about following clues to discover a solution. That's what science is about."

"I needed friends that summer, and the characters in _____ seemed to be my friends."

"The first time I thought the world of business might be exciting was when I read _____."

"My interest in writing poetry came from hearing Dr. Seuss read over and over to me."

Common Problem #4: "Should I Be Funny or Serious?"

You might as well ask: "Should I be short or tall?" It depends on you, what and who you are.

Seriously—or comically—it is quite all right to be humorous or funny in your essay. Humorous does not mean stupid. In fact, some lightness of tone probably succeeds; an overly solemn tone does not. But use some common sense:

• Be careful about poking fun at those things your college may take seriously. Admissions officers at a conservative Bible college may not relish a spoof of Genesis; those at a liberal arts college may be uncomfortable with a satire of intellectual life.

• Make certain that your humor is not merely an imitation of Chevy Chase or Woody Allen (although attention to good comedy may get your creative juices flowing). Demand quality from yourself in a comic essay, just as you would in a serious one.

• Remember that this is an essay, not a stand-up night club act.

• Don't use humor as an excuse for being destructive. Comedy is not synonymous with fault-finding.

• Some of the most successful humorous essays are ones in which the author shows that he or she can laugh at himself or herself. You make the important point that you can step outside yourself and look at yourself with some objectivity.

• Use humor as the means for saying something significant, not as a means of avoiding significance.

Common Problem #5: "I Said It All in the Rest of the Application"

The applicant here is wise. Don't repeat. If you've mentioned being president of the French Club in a list of activities, don't merely say that you held that office in your autobiographical essay.

Instead of repeating your record, tell your reader why you chose to do the things you did. Tell the reader what effect your experience had on you.

Your autobiographical essay should address issues not included on lists of honors, activities, etc. For example, your character, your values, your relationships with your family and friends, your interests outside of school, your experiences, are all possible topics.

You may have said that you were captain of the football team in another part of the application. Your essay may be the place to tell your reader the significance of this honor.

How did you feel when you became captain?

Was it what you expected?

How did it change your relations with people at school?

Was it a significant moment in your life?

Common Problem #6: "I Wrote Five Sentences. I Have Nothing More to Say"

Some people have difficulty developing what they write. Here's a sample from an essay by Alice, a high school senior applying to Southern universities. She has difficulty developing her ideas.

> Working at McDonald's last summer taught me three things. I learned how to work in a business environment. I learned to get along with different kinds of people. And I learned that earning money is hard work. Therefore, my job at McDonald's has helped me mature.

Alice has done good thinking. She's outlined three

important points, and she's suggested a cause-effect relationship. But she hasn't made her essay lively or convincing. She will do both by supporting her generalizations with details.

She needs to do two things:
1. Divide up each sentence to note key terms.
2. Interview herself about each term.

For example, in her third sentence she needs to think about two key phases: "learned to get along with" and "different kinds of people." The second term is easiest to think about: it is specific and concrete.

Her interview with herself might go like this:

Alice-Questioner: I said there were different kinds of people. What did I mean?

Alice-Interviewee: There was the manager, the three kids I worked with, and the customers.

A-Q: Were the customers all alike?

A-I: There were the Yuppy types at lunch from the office building next door and the jurors from the Courthouse across the street. We were at a bus stop, so people going crosstown would come in and want their orders fast. And the bus drivers would come in. They were regulars. They'd always joke with us. The office workers wouldn't though. Except once this stuffy legal secretary came in at the end of the summer; I knew just what she wanted, so I brought her her usual order even before she asked for it. Was she surprised! After that, she'd talk a little bit when she came in.

A-Q: What about the kids I worked with?

A-I: Well, some were really poor and needed the money. For some, it was just a way to get extras.

Sheila would spend every cent on Izods on Friday. It made a lot of kids jealous. Like Lydia; I think she was a single mother who dropped out of school.

A-Q: I said I learned how to get along with these people. What did I mean?

A-I: I sure didn't get along with George at first. He thought I was a snob because I was planning on going on to college, and I couldn't understand his Black English. But when I knocked over a set of shakes, he was the one who bailed me out.

Alice has now done the hard part: she's thought analytically about her experience. She's extracted the ore from the mine of her experience. She's well on her way not only to filling a sheet of paper, but to making her essay interesting. Convincing. Real. Thoughtful. She has thought of supporting information that makes her experience real to the reader and her claims persuasive.

Common Problem #7: "English Is My Worst Subject"

Everyone moans over the essay. The loudest moans come from scientists and mathematicians, computer experts and artists, student leaders and solid workers who perhaps don't combine interest in English or skill in English with their other strong points.

How handicapped is the applicant who is "not good in English?" The answer is complicated.

On one hand, several schools look for a correlation between English grades on transcripts and the quality of the essays. These schools expect a close relation between the student's grades in English and the level of writing on the application; one validates the other. Other schools find that some of their best essays come from students whose grades in English were average. The explanation? High school English courses develop many different skills in students. Some of these skills are essential to good essay writing. Others are not.

Will your English grades foretell the quality of your essay?

• Generally, students interested in writing will get good grades in English, and will write good essays.

• Many students are excellent observers of life, rational thinkers, and clear, articulate writers about their observations. They might not be interested in literature or in the study of grammar; they might not have been "good in English." Their essays will be promising ones.

• Some students will have difficulty with their essays. They are students who

are indifferent to language,

are uninterested in learning in or outside the class-room,

have few opinions or interests.

The best indication of success in the application essays—and success in college—is not your English grade. It is the lively, interested mind of someone who cares about his or her experience.

Common Problem #8: "Is It OK to Write on a Topic Different from the One on the Application?"

"My essay for Scripps is much better than this one for Reed. Can I substitute?"

"I'm applying to three schools. I wrote a good general essay about myself for one school. My second choice school asks for the most exciting event in my life—which I didn't include in the first essay. **My backup school wants me to describe the person who most influenced me. What am I going to do?"**

.The basic rule: follow directions. Read requests and instructions carefully. Ignorance—accidental or deliberate—of the instructions is not admired as creative. It *does* reveal itself.

Anecdotes circulate about those who ignored specific instructions and were admitted. One applicant to a women's college, tired of writing applications, responded to a request to describe herself this way:

"I am what I've done, and I've told you what I've done."

She was accepted. The question is, of course, was she admitted because she didn't follow rules, or in spite of so doing.

Hard and fast rules?

1. Note the requested form (usually an essay).

2. Note the requested length. Some schools allow applicants as many pages as needed; others give a word limit.

You do not have to count words exactly, but if your essay is substantially shorter than the requested length, you are suggesting that you are unable to develop an idea fully, that you lack intellectual substance.

If your essay is substantially longer than the requested length (say 20 per cent longer) you are asking the busy admissions office to put extra time on your application. Are you certain your essay is good enough to warrant the request? What if your reader does not read to the end of the essay? Will he or she miss something important?

3. Note the requested topic, and note the form in which it is presented. That is, the requests "Tell us more about yourself" and "Tell us how you would like to be remembered" are both asking for autobiographies, but the responses are to be couched differently.

Questions may vary from year to year. But the year in which you will be applying, the admissions committee chose questions to be answered. Schools are not flattered if you submit to one school an essay written for another school.

Can you adjust your essay from application to application?

In spite of what clothing stores tell us, one size does not fit all. But with a little tailoring, one size can sometimes be made to fit.

The same with essays. You can't palm off a single essay to fit a variety of questions. Sometimes you can tailor one essay to fit a variety of questions. At least you might be able to use one essay to simplify the task of writing another.

1. Check your best essay to see if it has the seeds of another essay in it. An essay about a summer job might yield an essay on an influential person—if one of your coworkers or your boss qualifies. Or an autobiographical essay on the problems of switching schools your senior year might be a good quarry for a response to "What was your most memorable educational experience?" An essay on a favorite book might yield an essay on an intellectual experience. Look at essays at the end of this book. Can you find another essay in each waiting to get out?

2. What was the purpose of your original essay? What impression were you trying to make? Were you trying to

show that you are smarter than your grades? Responsible? Interested in the arts?

You might want your second essay to have the same purpose, even if your topic is different. For instance, if you are showing the school you are a jock, an essay about a book or about your most significant experience could also show you are sports-minded.

If you are writing an essay in addition to the one autobiographical essay, decide whether you want to *emphasize a single quality or show another quality*. For example, if you were a jock in one essay, do you want to emphasize political interests in another? Virtuosos play well on one string; more often several strings sound better.

3. Can you write on a topic different from the one requested? Can you introduce a different topic? If you're asked to describe a book, don't blithely offer a movie review instead. *Unless* you have a genuine, honest and persuasive reason.

> "I'm a visual person, interested in the graphic arts, and so images mean more to me than words. . . ."
> "This movie was originally a book, but for several reasons the story became more meaningful when it was translated to another medium."

Such ploys are risky; think carefully about whether they are worth using.

4. Consider using the common application for schools that subscribe to it. (Avoid using it for schools that seem only to tolerate it, asking for additional information.) Use of the common application simplifies essay writing. However, some admissions officers note the sacrifice of the personal, individual interest reflected in the individual

school application. College counselor Dwight Hatcher suggests applications consider the analogy of the "Dear Student" or "Dear Occupant" letter.

5. If you have another essay or creative product you want the admissions committee to see, don't sacrifice it for the required essay. By all means consider submitting it in addition to the application, especially if it reflects a particular talent. It is entirely appropriate for the musician to submit a tape, a writer to submit a poem, an artist a drawing. Exception: Most admissions people say that science projects are not helpful; recommendations from knowledgeable sources about your scientific activity are better. Make certain that supplementary material is of good quality (tapes are clear, for example) and that the committee will accept your submission. (Will someone watch your video? See your slides?)

Wise applicants make every bit of supplementary material—even letters—count. Note the graceful letter that applicant Vincent Crespi writes:

> Just a quick word about my interview before you get to the application proper. I was nervous. I don't think that I came across as I should have (I'm not psychic, though). So if the application and the interview seem to be pointing towards different people, just consider the interview to be the cloudy window, and the application to be a better, although still imperfect, description. Best of luck in clearing the windows.

Common Problem #9: "I've Got to Get Hold of a Thesaurus. I Need to Put Bigger Words in My Essay"
"I'll never get admitted. My vocabulary stinks."

These applicants are both right and wrong.

They are right about the value of expanding vocabulary and the value of choosing the exact word in the essay. They are right in thinking that admissions officers will be impressed by someone who cares about language. And the readers will be impressed by the candidate who deals accurately with a big word representing a big concept—for example, the essay dealing with *Weltschmerz* at Central High School or analyzing the school's version of *Guys and Dolls* in post-structuralist terms. But these essays succeed not because their writers use $25 terms but because they can deal with the concepts represented by the words.

The applicants are wrong, however, in thinking they need "big words" to impress. There are good reasons that they are misled. Schools emphasize developing vocabulary and many of the tests applicants face measure control of vocabulary. However, the emphasis should be on the applicant's having a large vocabulary so he can choose the simplest and most accurate word to fit his meaning.

Virtually all educated people agree: good writers choose the simplest, shortest word that suits; good writers use long, exotic, obscure words only when they best express their meanings. And good writers make certain they use exotic words correctly.

Sometimes you need to find a better word than the one that pops into your head. The following writer, Jack, needs to search—perhaps in a thesaurus—for more precise language:

"My year as an AFS student was fabulous because I stayed in a fabulous city, Paris, where the food and hospitality were fabulous."

However, writing will sound phony and stilted—and the perceptions seem vague—if France suddenly becomes "scintillating," the food "quintessentially gastronomic," and the hospitality "compassionate and urbane." This

Francophile needs to do two things:

1. Find the adjectives that substitute for "fabulous" which are more precise, yet are simple and unpretentious.

2. Or, even better, not rely on adjectives. Rather, explain the qualities observed, relying more heavily on nouns and verbs, the strongest parts of the language.

The first rule: Make your language as precise as possible. Then choose the simplest precise terms.

Many student writers fear that simplicity will make their writing sound like baby talk or primer prose. But accuracy prevents that. "See Spot run" is not an accurate way for a teenager to tell someone to observe a dog—to look at, to watch, to glance at a dog scampering, gamboling, skipping, darting. The precise words in the preceding sentence will lift the passage from babyishness to mature, precise writing: you don't have to say—nor should you say—"Perceive the canine perambulate swiftly" to flaunt your vocabulary. Such pretensions work against you.

The second rule: Remember that precise writing is colorful and informative.

VI
THE ADMISSIONS OFFICE VIEW: COMMON MISTAKES— AND HOW TO AVOID THEM

Experienced admissions officers find their complaints are familiar ones. Many of the unsuccessful essays exhibit similar faults.

Following are comments from admissions officers. Will your essay be noted this way?

1. "Haven't We Read This One Before?"

Sometimes admissions officers get essays that are clones; they sound alike—they echo each other. Occasionally they raise the question of plagiarism, though not often. Usually the issue is lack of original thinking—or the product of lack of work. The applicants' hesitance to think and rethink their experience makes their essays sound alike.

But American 18-year-olds have similar experiences. No wonder they sound alike! Remember: many novels have similar plots. The material is not new. The point of view and the treatment are.

Realize that you will probably be writing on the same subjects as other applicants: experiences in Scouting, football, debate, summer jobs, AFS travels.

Realize that admissions committees have seen many essays in which:

> An AFS experience reveals that people are the same the world over;
> A summer job gives someone the first taste of responsibility;
> A disappointment makes the writer stronger.

You don't have to sound like other people. Your essay can sound unique.

Find a new perspective on the subject or take the old perspective and re-examine it so that you can provide an original treatment. Don't be satisfied with easy answers.

Use all the resources you have. Surely *Catcher in the Rye* helps you understand your own adolescence, but viewing your life only through Salinger's eyes makes your essay imitative. Look at your life through Salinger's eyes, but also through the eyes of your little sister, of a visiting AFS student, and most importantly, through your own eyes.

The subject need not be original. The thought need not be new. But each essay should be the product of fresh, original thought. Yesterday's fish and fish caught fresh from the sea look alike. The experienced nose can tell the difference.

2. "The Essay Writer Sounds Middle Aged" "I can't get the sense of the writer here." "This doesn't sound as though a high school student wrote it."

Too often, essays arrive lacking the sense of the writer's personality or youth. Such essays display ideas that seem hackneyed, or ideas that seem accepted without consideration, or ideas presented in stilted or banal language.

The cause? Often students are afraid to sound like the young people they are, and they drain the sound of their own voices from their work. They echo parents or teachers. Or what they've been told colleges want to hear.

Liveliness flees.

Conversational language vanishes.

Language associated with adolescence is eliminated.

Such writers have good instincts. They want to learn from their elders and to write correctly. But they need to reveal themselves in the essays, not to shroud themselves in the disguise of parents or teachers.

For suggestions about maintaining your own personality in the essay, see Chapters III and IV.

3. "This Writer Thinks He's Smarter Than We Are"

Two kinds of applicants draw this comment.

The first is usually determined to reveal his or her strengths, so determined that he or she exceeds all bounds of modesty. Convinced that only an Einstein or Mother Teresa will be admitted to college, he or she depicts himself or herself as one or the other. The essay charts triumphs, mastery of subjects and skills. Smarter than anyone in class or school, the writer sails through difficult situations. Not only is the past marked by successes, the future holds no problems.

The second type of student who draws this comment from admissions officers has a similarly simple view. This writer chooses a style that tends to be critical, cynical and sardonic. Rather than charting his or her own successes, this writer relishes other people's failings. Peers are stupid. Teachers "idiots." School is a "bore." This country's statesmen are "jokers." Other countries' "imbeciles." And so on.

Rules to remember:

1. You never climb very high by climbing over other people.

2. Don't hide your light under a barrel. But don't claim your light outshines the sun. Record your successes and abilities. But you also need to show you recognize the complexity of most endeavors. Realistically admitting your mistakes will validate your claims to successes.

4. "This Writer Doesn't Think He Needs College" "This writer doesn't think he needs our school."

If you are the sort of student who has a clear view of your future—the kind of life you will have, the kind of job you will have—you may have a good topic for an essay.

But if you are such a student, be cautious. Too often students like you write about college as though it is an obstacle to be overcome or a door to be gone through as fast as possible. Your essay might read:

"I look forward to going to Podunk College Business School because as soon as I graduate I will be on my way to making my first million."

Or:

"I have always wanted to be part of the construction industry. As soon as I leave college I will get a job in my father's business."

The admissions committee reader might ask: "How does college help the writer achieve his goals?" "Why does she need to go to college at all?" "Why does our school fit into his vision of education and training for his future?"

No school wants to regard its degree as merely a ticket to the next stage of life. You need to consider why the two or four years spent at school is significant. Then explain that to the reader.

5. "This Student Isn't Taking the Application Seriously"

"She doesn't seem to care about us. Where do you think she really wants to go?"

No school wants to admit an unenthusiastic student, a student who is indifferent. Applicants reveal real or apparent indifference by not taking applications seriously. Such applicants

• show little awareness of the peculiar character of the school to which they're applying,

• ignore the requested topics for essays,

• neglect to organize their essays carefully,

- write short, ill-considered answers,
- allow material that is off the topic to creep in,
- choose language haphazardly,
- neglect proofreading.

You can show the school that you take a serious interest in attending. Check your essays:

1. Do show that you know the school's special qualities.
2. Do answer the question asked or write on the topic assigned.
3. Do discuss fully the subject in the space allotted. Don't give up with arrows still in your quiver. Don't treat one issue when two are appropriate.
4. Do organize your material before your final draft.
5. Do eliminate peripheral material.
6. Do pay attention to language.
7. Do proofread—at least twice.

6. "He'll Need Our Remedial Program If We Admit Him"

"Her grammar is terrible."
"Accidental typos or mis-spellings?"
"Sloppy, haphazard."

Not everyone writes perfectly grammatical English or types professionally. Some bright, talented people—including college students—are terrible spellers.

If you know you have trouble with grammar, spelling or punctuation, ask a friend to look over your essay. That's not cheating, especially if you learn from your friend's suggestions. Rather, it shows awareness of some errors that need to be corrected.

Even if you have good control of grammar, spelling and punctuation, don't jeopardize your strength by neglecting to proofread.

Re-read once for the general sense of the essay.

Re-read a second time for the sense of individual sentences.

Proofread for mechanical errors.

Re-read again.

Allow time in between the re-readings so that you come to the essay fresh each time.

7. "[Yawn]." "OK, But Boring"

Give your reader a break. And maybe he or she will give you a break. Make your essay interesting, and maybe the school of your choice will be interested in you.

As we've said before, an interesting essay is not trivial or superficial or sensational. The depth of your thinking, the thoroughness with which you record observations, will keep a school admissions committee reader interested.

Following are some strategies to help make even a good, interesting essay better:

1. Check your opening sentence and opening paragraph.

Are they right on the topic? Don't start too far back. For example, an essay on how the Holocaust affected your family should not start with the history of the Jews; an essay on your founding of a community action organization at school need not chart all your extra-curricular activities.

Does the opening make your reader want to read on? Would you read an essay that starts out

"I have always thought that . . ."

or

"I was born on June 19, 1970,"

or

"My primary academic interest is . . ."?

2. Check the opening of each paragraph. Do all the paragraphs start the same way? Particularly, do they start with "I am" or "I was" or "I think?" If so, seek variety.

3. Whenever possible, improve your essay by being
   concrete,
   specific,
   particular,

rather than being
   abstract,
   vague,
   general.

Instead of saying,
   "I had trouble with teachers my freshman year,"
be specific:
   "I wanted to talk, and my teacher wanted me to listen,"

or

   "My teachers thought I would be just like my older brother,"

or

   "My teachers thought I should agree with them, but often I had different opinions."

Instead of saying, "I admire Bishop Tutu because he is a good man," define "good man." Tell why you think he fits your definition. Is he good because he lives by his religion? Because he acts on his beliefs?

Such specificity does two things for your essay:

1. It represents the complexity of your thought.
2. It keeps your reader interested.
4. Consider lightening up your essay with appropriate
   conversation
   anecdotes
   quotations
   proverbs
   allusions.

For example:

Conversation:

" 'A bicycle trip by yourself!' my mother exclaimed."

Quotations:

"Harry Truman said, 'If you can't stand the heat, get out of the kitchen.' Maybe. But if the only job available in the hottest summer on record is frying burgers, what would you do?"

Proverbs:

"I knew I shouldn't put all my eggs in one basket, but when I sent off applications . . ."

Allusions:

"I remember how hard it was to get students to line up for Hands Across America. I thought that was tough until I lined up pre-schoolers to go to the bathroom, wash their hands, and then eat juice and crackers."

Ancedotes:

Instead of telling that you put a frog from the dissecting lab onto your English teacher's desk when he was preparing to teach a Mark Twain story, record what happened.

Descriptions:

You could say, "My youngest uncle is different." But it is better to be specific. "My father and his two older brothers are corporate lawyers, but his youngest brother plays the guitar and slings hash at a diner." Then describe a family gathering. What do the brothers wear? What do they talk about?

Remember: you do not have to be sensational to make your essay interesting. But you have to give your readers something to focus on.

8. "Is This Our Application?"

Admissions officers respond this way if the applicant ignores the requested essay and substitutes another essay topic from another application. The reader can interpret your substitution in one of three ways:

1. "This person can't read directions." That's a poor recommendation for admission.
2. "This person cares more about being admitted to another school—the school for whom the essay was written—than to our school." If you're not enthusiastic about your admission, don't expect admissions officers to be.
3. "This person is lazy." (See number 1.)

Don't show up in tennis whites if you're asked to go swimming—even if you're a good swimmer. Don't breakdance if they're playing a waltz—even if you don't like the music. That is, if you want to be invited to the dance.

9. "This Essay Is OK. But It Is Not Outstanding"
"This doesn't help his chances, but it doesn't hurt either."

"Adequate."

Perhaps these are the single most familiar comments from admissions officers. One Yale admissions officer has said that the university receives only a few essays a year that are really dazzling, that really make the committee's spines tingle.

You have the best chance of making the reader sit up and take notice if you do the following things:

• Pay attention to your attitude toward your essay. If you are writing an essay just to fill in blank space, just to get the job over with, your essay may be adequate but it will certainly never be outstanding. Make yourself want to say something significant.

• Carefully heed
   advice from your English teachers
   advice from your college counselors
   advice in this book.

• Allow yourself enough time for the job.

At a minimun, what you want is an essay that does not hurt you. What you hope for is an essay that will positively help you, that will give you the edge in admissions. A good essay pays off.

SAMPLE ESSAYS AND COMMENTS

The following essays, reflecting varying styles, tones and approaches, were written by students who were admitted to at least one of the colleges they chose. Many of the writers were admitted to several schools.

These essays suggest the diversity of college freshmen. Most schools attempt to gather a varied student body. For admissions officers, selecting a freshman class is a little like choosing a crew for the maiden voyage of *The Enterprise*. On a four year journey, a crew composed of Dr. Spocks would be dull. The essay should make a case for the student's individuality, so he or she can join the diverse crew.

As you read these essays, put yourself in the position of the admissions committee reader: How would you respond to the applicant on the basis of the essay? At one private school, seniors are asked to estimate SATs and GPAs, and to imagine what the student writer is like. Are you able to make intelligent guesses about the essay writers' academic records? Interests? Reputations in school? You might ask the following questions:

1. Does the essay show the writer as an individual?
2. What characteristics of the writer does the essay reveal? Independence? Responsibility? Honesty? Maturity? Sensitivity?
3. What will the writer bring to the school community?
4. Does the essay note special talents and interests that would probably not be reported elsewhere on the application form?
5. Would the essay diminish a fine high school record or enhance a weak one?
6. Does the essay suggest the applicant's potential for success?
7. Does the applicant have a command of written English? Can the writer effectively communicate his or her ideas?

The following questions might lead to an understanding of why the essay created the effect you noticed.

1. What did you like or dislike about the essay?
2. Is the essay unified?
3. Does the essay's opening sentence or paragraph provoke your interest?
4. Is the subject interesting?
5. Is the organization logical?
6. Do you notice smooth transitions between paragraphs?
7. Are all assumptions and generalizations documented?
8. What should the writer have eliminated?
9. Are any essays unsuitable? Do they sound like recycled English papers?
10. Do you see any essays that reflect considerable thought and effort?

11. Why do words like "pretension," "insincerity," or "smugness" come to mind after reading certain essays, while in others writers appear confident, sincere, and knowledgeable?

12. Did the writer choose words carefully? Did he or she avoid clichés?

Writing the essay is hard work. Eventually, many students consider the experience—and the whole application process—a valuable learning experience, and a necessary rite of passage. Writers' evaluations of their own work vary. After only one year—from high school senior to college freshman—many students still view their efforts proudly. Others cringe when they re-read their essays. Some said: "It got me where I want to be. It must have worked. But I'd probably approach it differently today." Such students recognize that there is no perfect essay. The essay can always be improved.

Of more than 50 essays, only one has been shortened. A few writers wanted anonymity. If essays pointed to real people who might wish to remain anonymous, we substituted "Smith," "Jones," or "Abel" for their names. Colleges that prospective students raved about but didn't attend, we refer to as Generic U.

These essays allow you to see how others have approached the challenge. This should be your all-important first step in writing your own essay.

WRITING ABOUT JOB EXPERIENCES

Job experiences can often yield interesting essays. Keith Winkeler from Rice University employs an original poem within his essay to tell how being the "Party Man" at McDonald's has helped him understand himself. A student currently at the University of Pennsylvania, Mark Fishbach, tells of working in a community committed to the joys of scientific investigation at Woods Hole, Massachusetts. Aaron DiAntonio, from Clayton High School in Missouri and now at Harvard College, recounts his first nervous day on the job at a hematology research laboratory. The following essay about two friends starting their own neighborhood business was submitted to the Telluride Association Summer Scholarship Program. Duke's Mike Brown recalls how the experience of being a docent at the Philadelphia Museum's Rodin collection furthered his interest in the fine arts. The University of Virginia's Greg Downey relates the details of a near drowning and how that event made him realize that he could make a real difference in people's lives. His essay tells how his experience as a life guard helped him gain insight into the nature of responsibility. Finally, Vincent Crespi, applying from Andover Academy, uses dialogue in his discussion of the art of being a good tutor. Vincent is now at the Massachusetts Institute of Technology.

*   *   *

"Okay, where're all my party children? I need all the guests to come into the party room!"

Why do I work at McDonald's? Certainly, I need the money. But, why do I insist on hosting birthday parties instead

84

of just flipping burgers all the time? I like working with kids.
Why do I like working with kids? Because I enjoy making kids
smile and laugh. Why? Because. Because why? JUST
BECAUSE!

The Party Man

(Who is this guy? What is he doing here?)
"Hi there kids! Lend me your ear!"
(What's he saying? Is he talking to me?)
"I'm selling a party and a smile's the fee!"
(Boy, he's silly! I'm going over there.)
"You all take a seat. I'll take a chair."

Maybe I'm still a kid. I have yet to lose the sanity-
threatening inquisitiveness that nearly drove my parents crazy
13 years ago. And yet, I've lost much of my childhood naiveté.
The birthday parties, however, keep me from becoming "The
Cynic" or "The Pessimist." The smiling faces of 4-year-olds
can only be uplifting.

Or, do I like to play the clown? I enjoy playing with the children. It's not work. A feeling of accomplishment engulfs me as
my games and tricks brighten their day. I strain my creative
capabilities in an effort to individualize each party. No rules or
boundaries exist. I'm free to be me while bound to entertain
the children. I thrive on the challenge.

Hey there, mister! What is your name?
My name's Keith! Do you want to play a game?
Where are we going? What are we playing?
We're going over there and that's all I'm saying.
Here we are. Now what shall we do?
Just stand right there until I give you the cue!

They step into my world of McDonald's playland. Or, am I
stepping into their world of carefreeness? The "letting go" or

relaxation necessary for hosting a party helps me put events and situations of the past week in perspective. I have an easier time being honest with myself. My frustration at receiving a "B" on what I thought was an "A+" essay subsides. Or, an argument that I had with my mother suddenly seems utterly ridiculous. Once I place a situation in perspective, I have a much earlier time dealing with it.

> The games are done, they eat cake & ice cream.
> I sit back and watch them smile and beam.
> I am a little sad, for I won't see them again.
> But in a little while, I'll host another party of 10.
> How about the next one? I guess it'll be alright,
> Each one's different and hits a new height!

This "Holden Caulfield" characteristic of my life acts as a "catcher" for me. It keeps me from being "phony" and inhibits any fear of being different.

I no longer work at McDonald's, but I still express my "Holden"-ness at St. Louis U. High. After working at the freshman orientation, the moderator chose me to be a freshman homeroom advisor. Interacting with the freshman, I tutor one, go to a ballgame with another, or play pool in our rec room with several.

By doing this, I utilize my talents to benefit others.

— KEITH WINKELER

COMMENT: What could seem more predictable than an essay about working at McDonald's? But Keith gives it a lively approach, breaks it up with verse (making it look easy to read), and most importantly uses the experience to reveal something of his personality and his ability to understand himself.

*   *   *

This was it, the final straw. I could stand cleaning out the frog tanks, cutting one half inch pins in half, even scrubbing the incubator, but when my summer job called for me to wheel a cart full of hazardous waste to the disposal room, I faltered. It wouldn't have been so bad had not the bottle with the bold warning been broken, or the chemical disposal room been across the street, but unfortunately they were. I had my orders, and holding the unofficial title "Doer of Neurobiology Course Dirty Work" along with the official "Course Assistant", I wheeled the cart to the elevator.

In the corridor I could have sworn I saw my charge glowing. But the worst was yet to come, for situated directly on the only path open to cart bearers headed from my building to the Chem Room lay "the bump". Like a modern day Scylla and Charybdis, "the bump" had risen on many occasions to topple my payloads of water bottles and boxes. My heart raced as I slipped down the embankment at the base of which lay the fiendish protrusion. Frantically my feet sought purchase on the macadam, but to no avail. With a sickening lurch, the cart took flight.

The inevitable sound of the cart's impact was accompanied by the shattering of glass. Of course the bottle marked "Hazardous" had borne the brunt of the damage and now sported two openings instead of one. No one around me seemed to be concerned with the fact that I had just been the cause of a major environmental disaster. Even the people in the Chemical Room weren't that alarmed when I wheeled in my cargo. I guess the wind was blowing away from me because I've never suffered from any ill effects.

This was by no means the first time my boss had unwittingly almost caused my demise. I worked near an area that would make a geiger counter go wild. Almost everyday I had to deal with ancient autoclaves which, like giant pressure cookers, I thought would blow up. However, occasional exposure to hazardous materials and subjection to less than desirable jobs were more than made up for by exposure to the type of people and the atmosphere that permeate Woods Hole.

Quite simply, people in Woods Hole love their work. Sure students may take three hour lunch breaks to sit on the beach, but they routinely work until three in the morning. Learning is never a chore for them. Students are so excited about their individual projects and course material that they'll just sit and talk about last night's experiment more often than that night's party. But party they do. People enrolled in the neurobiology course have so much fun and feel so rewarded with their education that many return to take other courses. It is this inherent enthusiasm and dedication that make the people I encounter at work my role models.

Another thing I admire about Woods Hole is the atmosphere. It's not just the neurobiology course that is so enthusiastic, it's the whole community. Having a population largely associated with science, Woods Hole seethes with the spirit of experimentation, hands-on learning, and original thinking. This spirit permeates everything. From second grade until I was too old to go, I attended The Children's School of Science in Woods Hole. However, it was not just a few who took the courses there, rather it was the majority of the child population. Nobody saw it as "school". Instead, it became just a fun learning experience. Classes such as marine biology, botany, nature photography, and biological illustration all were presented in an enjoyable learn-through-doing format. It is this atmosphere of exhilaration and hands-on learning that I have come to love, a love that can't be tarnished by a few distasteful tasks.

—MARK FISHBACH

COMMENT: Mark captures our attention with an exciting narrative. More importantly, his subsequent description reveals that he shares the enthusiasm for science that marks Woods Hole. The essay makes his values and zest for science obvious.

* * *

This is great; this is fabulous, infinitely better than sweating over a grill at McDonald's or pushing a Toro for the city's Parks Department. I am going to be a biochemist-for-a-summer, working with Ph.D.s to expand the frontiers of knowledge. Well, I had better get to my boss's house; he is driving to the medical center for my initiation into the world of science.

"Aaron, good to see you. My wife is coming along too, because she needs the car today." How will I get home? I'll bet he is going to jog; he always jogs. I can't jog that far. "I'm going to jog home." Oh God. "You can ride the shuttle." I sigh with relief.

This ride will never end. Purgatory won't last this long. I have nothing to say. Thoughts of an entire summer feeling incompetent to join in conversation flash across my mind. A slight tingling sensation that signals the onset of perspiration attacks my temples. He mercifully turns on the radio, thereby avoiding those final excruciating minutes of strained silence. In the middle of an ad for the Bowl-a-Rama, we arrive.

"Let's forget the elevator and take the stairs." That figures, he jogs. As he bounds up the stairs ahead of me, the perspiration on my temple turns into beads of sweat, which I promptly wipe away with a free hand. As I pass floor after floor of hospital rooms I imagine that I must be the only sixteen-year-old in America spending his summer vacation in a breeding ground for communicable diseases.

"Let me introduce you to everyone in the lab. This is our doctoral candidate Neil, studying steroid induction in cancerous cells; Jeanie a specialist in (some unpronounceable field), and Peter, a molecular biochemist." I am a high school student who enjoyed his first year of chemistry, especially the day we made peanut brittle.

"Let me show you some of the things you will be doing, Aaron. One of your main tasks will be tissue culturing. This involves work with cancerous mice tumors." A bead of sweat instantly forms on my brow. "You will need to learn how to use this machine; it measures the radioactivity in the samples we use." My forehead spews forth sweat with this last comment, and two beads drop to the floor uncomfortably close to his electric blue jogging shoes. "Don't be concerned at all, this is all very low-level radioactivity. Safer than a day on the beach." Reassured, I look up at his face with a smile and see that this man, under forty years of age, is almost totally bald. I have already resigned myself to losing my mind, but not my hair.

As I prepare to leave he looks me straight in the brow and says, "Don't worry, by June they turn on the air-conditioning."

Well, they did turn on the air-conditioning in June, and I was able to join in conversation. In fact, all my sweat was unfounded. I came to understand my work, and soon after began to love it. I was treated well by my co-workers and am proud to say that I was able to design a few experiments on my own. I even considered taking up jogging. While I did not expand the frontiers of science to any great measure, I did acquire an intense interest in scientific investigation. I gained great respect for the mysteries of science, and anticipate a career as a biochemist. This summer job, despite its inauspicious beginning, was the impetus for my future educational and career plans. Who knows, as a biochemist I might do myself some good and discover a cure for sweating.

— AARON DIANTONIO

COMMENT: Aaron makes clear that he held a significant summer job related to his academic future, but he also impresses the reader by not taking himself too seriously. His humor, his recording of his very human reaction with which any reader can identify, make the essay appealing.

* * *

As my sophomore year was drawing to a close, I realized I needed to find some form of summer employment. Since I was only fifteen years old, my possibilities were limited by the distance I could reasonably travel on my bicycle. After wasting quite a few Saturdays asking about work at every conceivable area business, I realized that being fifteen not only meant that I couldn't drive, but that I couldn't work. Due to the recession and my young age, the possibility of being hired for a real job was nil.

Mercifully, I was not in this predicament alone. A friend of mine was also fifteen, and he had had no luck in finding work either. So with the spirit of Ragged Dick and Fearless Fosdick in our hearts, we decided to set up our own lawn work and general maintenance business. We typed up fliers detailing the myriad of menial labor tasks we would gladly do, and had a few hundred copies printed. We blanketed both his neighborhood and mine with our brochures and waited for the flood of calls to come rolling in.

It cannot truthfully be said that an avalanche of responses came in that first night, but we soon did get a trickle of business. Within a few weeks we seemed to have a job a day. We did lawn cutting, weeding, bush removal, outdoor and indoor painting, and even, for one very unsuccessful day, bricklaying. The only job we turned down all summer was the removal of a dead bird from a birdhouse some thirty feet off the ground. The acrophobia we both have precluded any possibility of accepting this job.

Our work was made more pleasant by the many hours of free time we had each day. I spent much of this time reading and generally enjoying the summer as it should be enjoyed. I doubt that if I had been a fry cook I would have had this luxury. I also enjoyed the money I earned, some forty to fifty dollars a week. While this would not have impressed John Pierpont Morgan, it pleased me greatly. Earning my own money gave me a feeling of independence and maturity. While I would hardly say this experience "made a man out of me," it certainly made me feel that I was headed in that direction. If nothing else, I have a few hundred more dollars socked away for college.

—ANONYMOUS

COMMENT: A nicely written, laid-back essay. The reader might feel cheated, though, because the tale seems to lack a point.

*   *   *

As a sixth grader growing up in the Philadelphia suburbs, I was fortunate to have participated in a unique school program. Realizing that I had a strong interest in art, one of my teachers arranged an independent project for me to become a docent for my classmates at the Philadelphia Museum of Art. This, she felt, would further involve me with art and would also develop my ability to speak before a group of my peers.

Because of the Philadelphia Museum's extensive Rodin collection and because I was very interested in sculpture, my tour focused on the life and works of Auguste Rodin. I prepared for my presentation for a period of three months. This included doing research at various libraries as well as frequently visiting and viewing his works at the museum. During the tour, I led approximately thirty sixth graders through the museum and tried to explain or interpret fifteen pieces of sculpture while also introducing facts about Rodin and his life.

As it turned out, my experience as a docent affected me in just the way my teacher intended. I learned how to express myself in front of my peers, and this helped me to develop more confidence in myself. As I have become increasingly aware of the differences in attitudes and opinions between me and others, this self-confidence has been important in learning how to deal with peer pressure. In the past, I was less willing to do as my own conscience and interests dictated; now I try to act in a manner more consistent with my own ideas.

My enjoyment of art has continued to grow because art allows me to express myself with great variety. As an artist, I view a subject and interpret an idea in any manner I choose. I have thus become further motivated toward working in the fine arts and have exhibited my artwork at local art shows and galleries. At the same time, I have also become aware of art as a means of communicating my ideas. This year, as the assistant editor of my school's national award-winning literary and art magazine, I am involved with the expression of ideas by playing a key role in deciding which articles, stories, poems, and pieces of art are to be included in the magazine as well as having an extensive influence on the magazine's production.

Intellectually, my past experience as a docent furthered my interest in the fine arts and art history. Emotionally, it did much more. It not only helped me to develop greater confidence in my own ability but also encouraged the growth of my individualism and independence of thought: it helped me become my own person. Six years after being a docent, the lasting effects of this experience are still present.

—MIKE BROWN

COMMENT: A careful, well-organized account.

* * *

I never believed that a person drowning would really look like the actors in the Red Cross training films that all lifeguards endured before certification. How or why anyone would float underwater waving their arms up and down without kicking or attempting to breathe was beyond my comprehension. Then again, maybe the Red Cross did know what they were talking about because the child in the diving tank closely resembled a textbook case of drowning. I pulled out the "sinker"—my first drowning person ever—without even thinking about it. "Pull outs"—rescues—never occur routinely but often enough to take most of the shock value out of a rescue (at least for the guards, not the victims). All of the training paid off; I simply dove in, grabbed him, towed him to the side, and the child left the pool a few pounds heavier with swallowed water but no worse off because of the accident. The child climbed from the pool under his own power, and I returned to my perch above the crowd until another guard in rotation relieved me.

Later in the evening, I realized what had happened, or rather, almost happened, and my thoughts turned back to the rescue. I always believed that "pull outs" were part of the job that I was paid to do although I seldom had to actually enter the water to rescue anyone. That night, however, the gravity of the incident began to unfold to me. The wide-eyed child had spent nearly twenty seconds in thirteen feet of water inhaling things for which he had no use. When I grabbed his squirming body, he had been DYING!

Now, I had been to funerals and wakes and had "encountered" death—but not like this. In all of my previous encounters death was a state of existence; I had never seen death as an action occurring in the present tense. This death was real to me. And it was scary because it was not peaceful and quiet like a body in a casket; it was frantic and screaming, and it punched me in the jaw just trying to save itself. I felt proud because I had, quite literally, saved someone's life. On the other hand, I felt the weight of responsibility descend upon my shoulders. I could no longer just sit over the pool, soak up the sun, and watch girls. If in a "moment of truth" I failed in some way, someone's body could wind up on the bottom of the pool. Success and failure never held such importance in my life. I could make a real difference in someone's life or lack thereof. The fact that individuals could make a profound impact on the world or the people in it—not just as a lifeguard—snuck up on me while I was confused and defenseless.

It was my first rescue of the summer, and there were more to come. The handful of rescues made me nervous, but they also left me happy and committed to the belief that my actions mattered. I can not be content with letting things just happen because I might be what stands between a child with a real chance for a good life and a little paragraph in the obituaries.

—GREG DOWNEY

COMMENT: Drama and reflection combine here.

* * *

I walk out of the steady New England rain and into the welcome warmth of my vine-covered red-brick dorm. Two at a time I climb the creaking stairs, carefully dodging the low, cracked plaster ceiling. Reaching the third floor, I take a left, stick my key in the rusty lock, and, with a flick of the wrist, enter my small, L-shaped room. Flopping a pile of books onto my cluttered desk, I sit down heavily and contemplate the night's work ahead.

A twist of the knob and my door opens. I look over my shoulder. It's Sam, physics book in hand.

"Hey Vinnie, man, you've got to help me in physics . . ."

Tutoring is an art, not a mechanical chore, a "feed me a question and I'll spit out the answer for you" type of process, but a very complicated effort. To be a good tutor obviously requires a good working knowledge of the subject involved, but you must temper this raw understanding with a real caring for the person that you are helping.

"How would you do a problem like this?"

"Uhhh." I throw myself back a year in time. "Oh yeah, first of all you . . ."

In order to tutor effectively, you obviously must have a thorough understanding of the subject. However, few people realize that the pendulum swings both ways; in trying to explain some subject, I often clarify the topic in my mind as well. For instance, right now I understand physics better than I did a year ago when I was taking the course. I've forgotten some of the details, but I have a better overview, a better overall feel for the basic concepts, an understanding which comes from explaining these ideas to students who are taking the course this year.

"How would you figure out this one?"

"O.K.," I pause to read the problem, "so what are we trying to find?"

"Uh, the distance the block travels before it hits the ground."

"O.K., so you want to find the *horizontal* distance that it travels. What do we know about the motion of the block left and right?"

"Well, it starts with a horizontal velocity of 4 meters per second."

"So what else do we need to find the horizontal distance if we already know the horizontal velocity?"

"The time?"

"Right, good. So time here deals with vertical stuff, how long it takes before the block to *vertically* reach the ground."

"O.K., so I guess I use this equation." (Points to $D = V_o t + \frac{1}{2} at^2$)

"Right . . ."

The smartest person in the world would be a horrible tutor if he or she lacked a real desire to help. The most satisfying benefit of tutoring is the good feeling I get inside when I help someone. I don't tutor just to satisfy some egotistical desire to prove that I'm better than other people (although I fear that the feeling does try to sneak in). I help for the sake of helping; I really can't explain my feelings any better than that.

"I don't see how that works."

"O.K., ummm," I shuffle through different ways of explaining the problem. "Well, if there's no force acting . . ."

Over the years I've developed some sort of subconscious "tutor's instinct." I can see different ways of explaining a problem and choose which method I feel will work best for whomever I am helping. This ability can work another way, too. I can explain things to myself much more clearly than I could before. This is just a fringe benefit, though. I tutor just because I like to tutor.

A few days later.

"Thanks a lot, Vinnie; I think I did pretty well on the test."

"Thank you, Sam."

—VINCENT CRESPI

COMMENT: The dialogue offers the readers' eyes some relief after blocks of type. And who could read this essay and doubt that Vincent has been a tutor and has thought about tutoring?

WRITING ABOUT TRAVEL AND LIVING ABROAD

Carla Power, a student at Yale, answers a common admissions question: "Tell more about yourself as a person." Carla charts her own development by showing how her attitudes toward living abroad have changed. Michael Armbruster of Washington University's School of Business writes of a church-organized trip to Florida, telling what that experience meant to him. Finally, Vilashini Coppan reflects upon her South African Indian heritage in an attempt to understand the present political situation. Vilashini is now a student at Yale University.

* * *

The globe seems to me to be very small and very traversable. I have spent half my life abroad with my family, on Fulbright and sabbatical years in Iran, India, Afghanistan, Egypt, and Italy, with summers in Europe and Mexico. Half my life I have roamed around the world via third-class transport, equipped with bedraggled luggage and an alarmingly blasé attitude toward transatlantic flights. Intermittently, I return to suburban St. Louis, to Clayton, an exceptionally stable, solid community.

Now, with post-pubescent overconfidence, I want to see more of the world. After university, I hope to join the Peace Corps and am considering careers abroad. I feel ready for undiluted exoticism. But it was not always so.

It was through literature that I was first able to be comfortable abroad. From the age of five, I began to fill the hours spent travelling with books. Though I loved to travel, I needed the buffer of literature between myself and the heady world. Most children read for escape; I read for stability. Books cut the exoticism of my life. They neutralized the strange places I visited, making them less so. At seven, when I went to see Mount Everest with a group of flower children, I read Enid Blyton boarding school stories. In Afghanistan, while Soviet MIGs scattered bombs over Kabul in the first leftist coup, I read *Charlotte's Web* aloud. Only when I returned to my Missouri apartment would I read adventure stories or books on the places I had been. Literature was a tool to help me live abroad. It served to bundle together the scattered bits of my image of the world, to connect my suburban existence with my world traveller one.

At seventeen, I read no longer as a stability tactic, but as a survival tactic. That is, literature is not only a way to retreat from the world but to complete and to understand my own. I read Tom Wolfe to appreciate America and Ruth Prawer Jhabvala to understand India.

My exposure to different countries from an early age has helped me to feel at home in the world. When I lived in Iran and Afghanistan, I was so young, and the cultures so alien, that I needed to be a part of a community of Westerners with whom I could bake chocolate chip cookies and attend the schools' baseball games. As I grew older and more secure in the world, my foreign experiences became, indeed, more foreign. I became less an expatriate and more a resident of the country I stayed in. The past three summers spent in Mexico, I took classes designed for Mexicans at the national arts institute—Instituto Nacional de Bellas Artes. The folkloric dance class, which I took for two summers, was full of ambitious young people from ranches, studying for dance teaching certificates. I was a novelty, lacking their sense of rhythm and their mastery of Spanish. Yet I soon belonged. I also volunteered at a summer school for handicapped children of Guanajuato state. Two days a week, I would help take the children on day trips around the area: picking *garambullios* in the hills, or teaching them to swim in nearby hot springs. Initially, I was apprehensive of playing Lady Bountiful, the stereotypical, well-meaning foreigner who self-consciously tries to help in Western terms, but fails due to cultural differences. But I soon realized that, in the specialized setting of the school for the handicapped, cultural differences were not a problem. The children were so estranged from people in their own culture that their relations with me differed little from those with Mexicans.

That summer was the pinnacle of my foreign experiences. Through my volunteer work and my dance class, I approached being a member of a foreign community. I no longer needed to tote along Enid Blyton to cushion the exoticness of it all.

Making a life for myself in a small Mexican town indicates my self-sufficiency abroad. Outside my own country, my independence rivals anyone's. I have long navigated myself around European and Asian metropolises on public transport. Yet in my own country, I have yet to learn that skill so integral to suburban maturity: driving. I have achieved fair fluency in four languages, yet I have never held a long-term paying job. My development has been upside-down from that of other Midwesterners.

I find myself weighing the values of Clayton, Missouri, much more heavily than do my peers: considering, for example, whether the American work ethic is as immutable as it may seem to many of my friends. Likewise Clayton serves as a basis for examining life abroad. Coming from a community where half the girls aspire to being surgeons, and the other half to being corporate lawyers, I was surprised to find that the Italian girls in my class at St. Stephen's School in Rome had no career plans. Even the brightest and most competitive would cling to the traditional aspirations of marrying well and raising a family. I have come to realize that cultural gulfs are the norm, but that the individual can bridge them.

At times, I feel a sense of loss at not being able to discover the world along with my peers. I cannot let "worldly" disintegrate to "world-weary." Yet no matter how broad my travelling experiences have been, they are in no danger of limiting me. The world still lies before me. Like the speaker in the

Frost poem, I have miles to go. Miles of travelling, of reading, and of thinking.

—CARLA POWER

COMMENT: The temptation here is obvious: Carla could have quit after recounting exotic tales of Afghan coups and trips to Everest. Instead, she subordinates travel stories to the charting of her own development. And she pays attention to an activity she will continue in college: reading. Carla has written a complicated essay, one that is interesting, and one that fulfills the application essay's main purpose—introducing the writer to the reader.

* * *

To think of an incident that was significant enough to alter my lifestyle is not an easy task, but one particular experience does come to mind. This event was a two-week excursion to Florida that I made two summers ago with a group of high school people.

The trip was organized by the Archdiocese of Belleville and was offered to private high school students in the bi-state area. The theme of the vacation was to do something that you had never done before, and on this particular trip, skin-diving filled that requirement. But the skin-diving turned out to be snorkeling (which we had all done before) and was by no means the most important event on the itinerary. Rather, the sharing of everything with (at first) total strangers, the being away from home, the contact with different types of people and the feeling of being independent were the high points of the trip. I feel that experiencing these new phenomena made me more susceptible to the ideas of others, more comfortable when becoming acquainted with strangers, more understanding of the lifestyles of different cultures of people, and more independent. Buying goods from Cubans in Fort Lauderdale and poor Bahamians on Bimini was a great learning experience. It made me understand how desperate they were and how much a few dollars meant to them. Likewise, the coexistence with people from other schools, especially with those from farming communities, was rewarding. It showed me how drastically different people could be even though they lived just fifty miles away. But by the end of the trip, I discovered how similar we really were.

Finally, I took home a great deal of pride and independence after being unchaperoned in the exciting and sometimes dangerous city of Fort Lauderdale, the sparsely populated city of Bimini, and the magical city of Disney. This taught me to break away from the comforts of home and get involved and explore our fast-moving and exciting world.

—MICHAEL ARMBRUSTER

COMMENT: Clear and well-organized, this essay might be more compelling, though, if Mike gave us evidence of the way his views had changed and if he substantiated some of his generalizations more specifically.

*   *   *

As a South African native who has lived in the Western world for the past fifteen years, I have been obliged to consider myself as a melange of two entirely different cultures and societies. Although I have spent most of my life living in Australia, Canada, and the United States, I am nevertheless constantly exposed to my ethnic heritage both in my family life and via my regular visits to South Africa. Since my family and I lead an essentially isolated life outside South Africa, we return every two or three years in order to visit our relatives, all of whom reside there. I have returned to my native country five times, but I believe that it was only on my most recent trip, one year ago, that I was mature and perceptive enough to appreciate the full complexity of my heritage. As a South African Indian, I am a product not only of Indian culture, but also of the Black, Coloured, and White Afrikaaner traditions. Clearly, the South African nation represents diversity both socially and culturally. It is a country of perpetual paradox; of beauty and repression, poverty and wealth, advancement and degradation. During two previous visits at the ages of nine and eleven, I was unable to comprehend the multiplicity of this country, and therefore felt a need to stratify, label and judge South African society. At that particular time I condemned my relatives for living under a blind apartheid regime, while perceiving myself as a member of the flawless process of Western democracy.

However, last year I recognized that it is impossible to believe dogmatically in the pristine qualities of one country while expecting to understand another country, both politically and socially. Although I refuse to condone the horrific practice of apartheid, I have realized that one cannot condemn an entire people as one may condemn a particular policy. The very insularity of the South African policy of racial discrimination appeared to demand defiance in the form of an open mind. It is a critical error to judge anything without first attempting to understand it. In order to protect the human integrity which is being violated in South Africa, it seems that one must approach the issue itself with integrity. In effect, by viewing the issue of injustice with a previous personal bias against one side, one negates the very attempt to conquer injustice.

Thus, last year I endeavored to comprehend South Africa's political system and global position. I also spoke with South Africans of various races in order to ascertain their opinions regarding the governmental system. This knowledge, in addition to my position as a foreigner, enabled me to view the issue of apartheid in a wider perspective. However, since I was a non-white foreigner, I was never permitted to divorce myself from the actual practice of apartheid. Having experienced flagrant racial discrimination, I feel that I am better able to understand the nature of prejudice and the emotions which it engenders. Finally, apartheid ceased to be an abstract concept and became a reality to me.

My attempt to achieve integrity in my opinions also extended to my views regarding America. Last year I discovered that I was prepared to reject the concept of a flawless nation, and to discuss the faults and virtues of the American system of justice and government. My interaction with South Africans of various races has given me a different, somewhat more objective perspective on America and on the national image. The South African media appeared to concentrate heavily on the existence of prejudice and racial conflict in America, supposedly a nation of pure equality. This viewpoint caused me to look beyond the issue of apartheid toward the fundamental issue of prejudice itself. Obviously, pure equality does not exist since bias and partiality encompass the totality of human experience. Policies such as slavery, the caste system and apartheid are simply the appalling outer manifestations of such personal biases. Perhaps society must first destroy these tangible forms of injustice in order to begin to confront the actual inner nature of human prejudice.

My South African experiences have obliged me to examine both my ideals and my cultural customs. By spending six weeks in South Africa last year, I experienced the process of tradition. Many South African families comprise four or more generations, thus creating a linkage system by which to propagate customs and beliefs. The comprehension of the origin and continuance of Indian culture will assist me in the integration of my ethnic tradition and my present life in Western society. Moreover, by considering the differences between South African and American culture, I am now better able to comprehend the nature of my parents' struggle to preserve their traditional religion, morals and way of life while living in a

Western nation. Ultimately, I have realized that I cannot embrace either South Africa or America, either my heritage or my future. Rather, I must attempt to fuse these two cultures, and to bring the wisdom and experiences of each to the acknowledgement of both as an integral portion of my identity.

—VILASHINI COPPAN

COMMENT: No tricks. No sensationalism. The essay makes demands on the reader as it clearly made demands on the writer. But what better representation of oneself than an essay that deals with complex issues in a thoughtful manner. Vilashini's subject is compelling and interesting, and her discussion of her changing ideas makes the essay impressive.

WRITING ABOUT ACADEMIC INTERESTS

Michael Millender of the Paideia School in Atlanta, now at Duke, writes of his love of history and his involvement in historical preservation. Harvard student Nicole Fitchner relates her experiences participating in the Georgia Governor's Honor Program, particularly the benefits of a summer of intensive conversational French. A Wisconsin student addresses the question of his future educational goals by highlighting two of his favorite subjects, history and biology. Steven Cohen, in writing his admissions essay to Washington University's School of Business, tells of his early interest in finance and the stock market. A student at the California Institute of Technology, Rob Grothe, analyzes the significance of being ranked first in his high school class. Todd Wilcox of the Heritage High School in Littleton, Colorado, now at Duke, briefly tells of his main academic interest, science. Another Duke student, Carr McClain, discusses his academic interest, computer science. Carleton College's John Liberstein, reflects upon writing the admissions essay itself. Angela Giles of Evergreen, Colorado, tells of her reasons for wanting to pursue a business career. Angela is now a student at Washington University. Finally, David Cowan's essay draws upon his religious formation to make observations regarding the apparent dichotomy between science and religion. David is currently a student at Harvard College.

*   *   *

When I was a shy, little eighth grader, a social studies teacher asked me if I would like to enter a paper in a statewide program called Georgia History Day. I said that I would. From that short conversation five years ago developed one of my greatest interests and the source of my favorite activities: history. Georgia History Day was great fun. I enjoyed the movies, the speakers, and especially the pleasure and satisfaction of winning the essay contest. In fact, I was so encouraged that I entered again as a freshman and have returned every year since.

I suppose my first exposure to the excitement of history was when I was a little child reading a comic book version of the Bible. The idea of people existing before me who dressed, spoke, and lived differently from me was intriguing. This same fascination continued to spur my interest even ten years later as I prepared my History Day entries. As my historical interests became more sophisticated, I began looking not so much for the differences between the world of the past and society of today but for the similarities between the two and the ways in which the past has influenced and shaped the present. I also began to enjoy doing my own historical analysis, using primary sources whenever possible.

The challenge of doing my own work with the original documents, along with my interest in Atlanta's past, led me to do a great deal of inquiry into early Atlantans and their role in developing the city. I have enjoyed researching individuals such as Hoke Smith (a governor whose inflammatory speeches led to the Atlanta race riots of 1906) and Joel Hurt (Atlanta's premier turn-of-the-century builder whose neighborhoods and early skyscrapers still grace the city). For my entry in the German-American Week Essay Contest, I researched Atlanta's early German-Jewish settlers. This hardworking, dynamic group's contributions to Atlanta included the city's first hospital, its first public schools, and its literary and theatrical institutions. The group impressed me because of its remarkable achievements as well as the copious records it left behind—a historian's dream. The fact that the nineteenth century German Jews' influence can still be felt made studying them even more enjoyable and interesting.

My participation in history-related activities has not been limited to doing independent research and reading. I have interned at the Atlanta Preservation Center, a non-profit organization committed to preserving the city's past and educating its citizens about it. I am presently creating a catalog of historic homes and buildings in Atlanta for reference use by the Center and the general community, and I help organize walking tours of architecturally significant residential and commercial city districts. I have really enjoyed this work; not only have I learned more about my city's past, but I have had the privilege of aiding people who are working to save Atlanta's built heritage.

History has been so important to me that I know my interest and involvement will continue for many years to come. I look forward to exploring it both in study and in action on the university level.

—MICHAEL MILLENDER

COMMENT: The subject of history, including specific references to Atlanta's history, keeps this essay from being unduly centered on the writer. Michael's consciousness of the causes and effects of his interest in history remind the reader of the student applying for admission. Michael unifies two aspects of the essay to make an effective presentation.

*   *   *

Last summer, I spent six weeks in the most intense learning and growing experience of my life. I was selected, along with 199 other high school junior and seniors, to participate in the Georgia Governor's Honors Program. This program provides an opportunity for promising students to spend six weeks studying a major field of interest with the help of the best faculty members in the state. To qualify, each student must be recommended by a high school teacher, write an essay, and pass through a series of interviews.

I chose to qualify in French, and after two grueling interviews "en français," I received the magic acceptance letter. I was excited, but a bit apprehensive, at the thought of being away for six weeks, stranded on the isolated campus of North Georgia College in Dahlonega, with a crowd of talented high school students and teachers whom I didn't know.

For four hours each day, six days a week, we studied in our major interest area. The first day, I found myself sitting in a classroom with thirteen other French-speaking students. Everyone was silent and afraid to speak. As the teacher began to address us in fluent French, I felt a sudden pang of terror. I wondered how I had gotten there, for I could not, at that moment, remember a single word of French. Two students began to strike up a conversation in French with the teacher, and I managed to smile, but underneath, I was terrified.

Somehow I survived the first few sessions, and over the next six weeks, my fellow classmates and I progressively became immersed in French. I never knew whether our teacher even knew English, for she never spoke a word of it, nor did anyone else. I finally was able to understand all that was spoken, and I unconsciously began to think in French. The atmosphere in the class was always intense, filled with the growing confidence of each student. The different levels of ability provided depth and interactions among classmates, and subsequently, friendships grew closer. We learned grammar, literature, and French culture through games, books and the sharing of personal experiences and came to know each other more than we knew anyone else. By the end of the program, we had developed our own inner world which we entered each day when we walked into the classroom. Yet, even out of the classroom, we all spoke only French with each other. In those four hours each day, we lived in our own French world.

This experience helped me to learn a lot more about myself. I actually could watch my self-confidence grow each day with each new accomplishment, and I began to share more of myself with others. I realized how much could be expressed through a foreign language, how much more than in English. Besides simply learning French, I learned about the art of self-expression, about the complexities of self-esteem, and about the composition of human relationships.

—NICOLE FITCHNER

COMMENT: Details make this account of an intensive language course seem real. The last paragraph offers tantalizing generalizations about the experience. The explanation of those generalizations would have been interesting indeed.

*   *   *

A question concerning my future educational plans strikes close to my heart. I have spent countless hours pouring over the different college guide books, speaking to admissions officers who visited my school, and discussing the subject with my family and friends. The only conclusion I have reached is that I'm glad I am a junior and have another year to decide. Am I interested in the traditions of Harvard, the reasonable tuition of Rice, or the 8,800 rolling acres at Palo Alto? The veritable smorgasbord of quality universities across the country makes my mind reel and my mouth water.

I am greatly looking forward to college and I am hoping for many new experiences. I would like to sit around a table at the student union and debate the defense budget with those on my left and school prayer with those on my right. I would like to wander through a library with 10 million volumes and actually find the book I was looking for. It would be exciting to go into a science lab and use an electron microscope and a mass spectrometer, if there are actual uses for a mass spectrometer. But most of all, I want to grow and change at college. I hope to meet interesting people and encounter new ideas. I am enthusiastic in regard to learning and I love a healthy discussion. I also am interested in a school with an active drama department, since I have enjoyed participating in various plays throughout my high school career.

My education should be a balance between science and humanities with a slight preference toward the sciences. A list of my humanities courses would undoubtedly be dominated by history, a subject that fascinates me. I have not yet found a favorite field in science so I would be sure to sample them all. Whatever courses I do take, I would hope not to be buried in a class with two hundred other students. I seem to benefit most from a small group setting where discussion and interaction with both the professor and other students are possible. In any case, a room containing more than fifty students all with papers and books must be a fire hazard.

As far as careers go, I have made even fewer decisions. If I were independently wealthy I would love to be a history teacher, feet propped up on my desk, discussing Jackson's Bark War with a group of interested students. However, since I have teachers for parents, I know that the teaching profession is not very stable and does not offer a great deal of financial security, something I seek. The one career that encompasses these points and most interests me at this moment is medicine.

My choice of medicine amazes my parents who remember me nearly fainting at the sight of blood at the age of three, but my nausea has been overcome by two events. First, I took a biology course with a teacher who inspired me with his enthusiasm and love for the subject. A particular experiment that made a great impression on me involved the dissection of a mouse. When I peered inside this creature I was awestruck by the complex system of miniature organs and bones and muscles that made that mouse a living creature. While I had known from my earliest days that "the hip bone's connected to the leg bone," it was a powerful experience to actually see this with my eyes. From that day forward I have seriously considered a career in medicine. The other episode that made me consider medicine was an interview I did for English class with a neighbor, a research doctor at Washington University. He spoke of the freedom he enjoyed in planning his days, and his great satisfaction he received from completing successful experiments and learning new facts about the inner-workings of a cell. His job encompassed the best of all possible worlds; the freedom of a flexible schedule, the satisfaction of success, and, of course, financial security. These two events piqued my interest in medicine, especially research medicine, and have most influenced any career possibilities I have considered.

As I look to the future I am excited by the many varied experiences I imagine that I will enjoy. For the Great Gatsby the attainment of the dream destroyed it, but I doubt this will happen to me. Yet even if it does, the fun of the anticipation I am enjoying right now would make it all worthwhile.

—ANONYMOUS

COMMENT: No admissions officer could read this essay and doubt that this applicant has thought about what he or she is getting into. In each paragraph, the topic sentence is expanded by precisely recorded particulars. No vague abstractions, no empty generalizations here.

*   *   *

I leafed excitedly through the business section of *The New York Times* and found, to my astonishment, that my first venture in the stock market was a success. I was now a bona fide entrepreneur!

How did my interest in the stock market begin? Last year I had the chance opportunity to accompany my father's friend, a prominent stock specialist, onto the floor of the New York

Stock Exchange. This experience opened the door to a new dimension in my life. I was filled with awe and intrigue as I watched the frenzied activity. Millions of dollars traded before my very eyes. When I went home that night, I knew I wanted to be part of that fascinating world.

My first impulse was to withdraw my hard-earned savings, squirreled away from summer jobs, and quickly invest them in the market. However, I realized that I had no knowledge of stocks or investments to guide me. Consequently, I began to research what factors caused stocks to fluctuate in value. I read the *Wall Street Journal, Barron's Magazine,* and I watched the financial reports on television.

Through my research I acquainted myself with the nature of a number of stocks. More importantly, I developed my own set of trading guidelines. One of my most important rules is to be cautious of "inside" information or tips. Another important rule I follow is not to go against the trend. For example, if oil prices go down, do not buy oil stocks. Buy into a field that will be affected by the change in price; buy airline stocks because airlines depend on oil. Most people who buy a stock think in terms of how much they are going to make. Instead, they should ask themselves how much they are willing to lose. Since I could not afford big losses, I decided to sell my stocks if their value dropped by 5%.

My rules and regulations were comforting until the day came for me to actually invest my money. Now, my moment of truth was at hand. After much deliberation, I decided to buy Rockwell International which was selling at 24 1/8. I could not believe it; I had just spent the quickest $1,000 of my life! For six weeks my apprehension mounted. Each day, the moment I arrived home from school, I rushed for the financial page to check my investment.

My story has a happy ending. Rockwell International went up to 28 ¼. Did I rush to Wall Street looking for immediate employment based on my first success? Of course not. On the contrary, I became painfully aware of how much more I would need to know to be able to function in the financial world. I had entered a new world—yet, I had only taken one small step. Now, I look forward to my college years so that I can prepare myself for a future in the world of finance.

—STEVEN COHEN

*   *   *

I am presently ranked first in my junior class. Class rank is intensely competitive and can change quickly. First. That is to say, I have the highest grade point average next to my name. Ten percent of my life's activities, about 870 hours of classes over the course of a 8760 hour-long year, are numerically better than 245 other juniors at SLUH.

To me, in a broad sense, this is not especially significant. I wish that I fared better in the other 90% of my life. (I guess we always want what we don't have.) Looking at myself, I do not think "Robert Grothe . . . first in the class at SLUH," although I sometimes find that many others who I see at school identify me in that way—as if my nose were two feet longer than theirs and my feet twice longer than normal and pointed at a 180 degree angle with respect to each other. It's depressing when I am dismissed by others who think of me as a "book worm" or an "egg-head" or a "brain," placing me within a category which they feel is unattractive or simply "strange."

These same people are the ones who unknowingly comment, "If I only had your grades . . ." to which I continue to myself, ". . . then you would be expected to maintain those grades. Good luck!" Many are incapable of realizing that life does not become easier given more intelligence, just a greater challenge, as well as additional pressure. Often, I feel that even my close friends think that life is easy for me and are unable to realize that I deal with similar problems in school with respect to keeping up with work, etc, etc, yet, for me, these problems are intensified by the expectations that others impose upon me and that I begin to impose upon myself. I serve, at my own expense, as the measuring-stick by which they gauge their performances. They laugh when I worry about a B +, forgetting that I do not measure my performance against theirs, but against that which is expected of me, internally and externally. My only academic measuring-stick is the performances of the past, and beyond that, perfection—a lot like banging one's head against a brick wall. My situation reminds me of the fate of Sisyphus, condemned to perpetually push a boulder up toward the top of a huge mountain. The further he pushes, the harder it becomes to proceed, yet to stop would be fatal.

My father incessantly reminds me, "Uneasy lies the head that wears a crown," quoting Shakespeare's *King Henry IV, Part 2*. I cringe every time he says that although I know he's right. At SLUH, academic competition is especially intense and there are some who resent being just behind me in the quest for the top grade point and psychologically take aim at me, as if to shoot me down with frigid remarks or even colder unspoken glares.

It may seem as if I feel bitter about school or paranoid about being first and falling. I enjoy school, but quite honestly, I am still concerned with class rank, to an extent, yet somehow maturity has shifted my perspective and values. My goals had always been to achieve academic honors, while at the same time, maintaining the most demanding curriculum. I see this equally important now—taking all available honors, advanced courses, and even advanced mathematics courses at a local university—yet this year I am seeing school as more than just a classroom as I become more active in the extracurricular side of school. I have continued my participation in cross country, become active in the writing and production of the school's weekly newspaper, am editor of the French section of the school's foreign language newspaper, an editor of the literary magazine and president of the Math Club.

I have since realized that being truly first means more than academics; it means being a well-integrated person and reaching out to help others. I have become more accessible to my fellow students in conversation and simply more friendly around school (not that I ever felt aloof, but I am plagued with a bad case of shyness). As intelligence is a gift, I have tried this year with great sincerity to use this gift for the benefit of others, as well as myself. I sometimes refer to my phone as the "Chemistry Hotline" alluding to the numerous calls which I receive the day before a lab is due or a test is scheduled. I am proud that a lot of people call me for help because it indicates to me that I am, to some degree, successful in my attempts to help others and not to mind doing so. I have noticed that many of the same people who had previously thought me as "strange" are gradually becoming those I call my friends.

—ROB GROTHE

COMMENT: Cleverly done. No reader will forget that Rob tops his class. And Rob both relieves himself of the attack that he is boastful—and shows the analytical turn of mind that must have helped him get high grades—by questioning the importance of the distinction.

*   *   *

The sciences have served as the core of my academic interests. The development of this interest can be traced to my early years in school, where I seemed to have had an insatiable desire to learn how things worked and why they appeared as they did. I can still remember the many hours I spent developing a model of a human cell out of Christmas ornaments, marbles, springs, and for the final touch, the contents of three tubes of Aquafresh toothpaste that served as the endoplasmic reticulum. As I progressed through school, more sophisticated projects and higher academic emphases continued to contribute to my fascination with the sciences. In high school, advanced placement biology and advanced placement chemistry have been two of my most challenging and interesting courses. These two classes have not only stressed the scientific theories, but they have also opened my eyes to the practicalities of science. Of particular interest to me has been the chance to participate in extra laboratory work and independent research projects.

In addition to my work in school, I received a scholarship to attend the Frontiers of Science Summer Institute at the University of Northern Colorado for eight weeks last summer. Here, taking organic chemistry, biology, computer science, and energy science in a college atmosphere, I was intrigued by the applications of science. Consequently, I have discovered that my focus in the scientific realm rests not on the formulation of theoretical concepts, but on the implementation of the theories.

Although I am definitely science-oriented, I have also developed a real appreciation for literature, especially English literature. Whether I am reading about Beowulf or Big Brother, Heathcliff or Henchard, I enjoy the powerful, yet mystical, nature of the English novel. I see my reading as a humanistic outlet not present when I'm dealing with the stark realities of science. Hence, I believe that my literary interest is a counter-balance that allows me to relate to others more effectively.

— TODD WILCOX

COMMENT: A straightforward statement of his interests. This account is distinguished by Todd's ability to load each sentence with precise information. This short essay convinces as a vaguer, more general one would not.

* * *

For the past five years, my primary hobby has been computers. My interest was sparked by my grandfather, who gave me his old machine when I was twelve. I bought several books about that computer and, over the next three years, taught myself the BASIC language, becoming a fairly proficient programmer. I achieved my skill without ever taking a formal computer course.

On my sixteenth birthday I received from my grandfather a new and far more powerful computer with disk drive and printer. With this new system I have not only continued to use BASIC, but I have begun recently to learn, on my own, the computer's machine language.

My first formal training in computers came after my junior year when North Cross sent me to the Governor's School for the Gifted at Virginia Tech. Governor's School provided my first opportunity to use a mainframe university computer. I began learning the Pascal language at Tech, and I have continued my study of Pascal in an advanced computer course at North Cross this fall.

Computers are a giant force in our society today, but by the time I leave college, the areas of their dominance will have increased markedly. A knowledge of the machines will be essential in many industries and will be a tremendous resource in the field of medicine, which I hope to enter. One need not aspire to be a professional computer programmer to choose the science as a college major and benefit from it in many of the practical activities of adult life.

—Carr McClain

Comment: The chronological organization works very well in this short account of a growing and developing interest.

*   *   *

"Have you written your essay yet?" Quite possibly, these are the six most feared words in the English language among high school seniors. Some of the most rational and intelligent teenagers across the country become sniveling incoherents once they realize that they are through with listing athletic activities, parents' names, and potential majors. It's time to play hardball, gang! Get out those Smith-Coronas and describe what accomplishment means to you and if necessary, please attach extra pages.

My only question is why? Why must colleges ask students to write an essay? And sometimes, it's not just one. Just the other day, I saw my good friend hunched over in a corner, weeping profusely. I stopped to see what was wrong and he didn't even speak to me. He merely gave me a copy of Dartmouth's application and after closer inspection, I discovered that it had eight. My first thought was that it had to be a typographical error or that Dartmouth's director of admissions was one of Attila the Hun's reincarnations. Unfortunately for my friend, I was wrong on both counts.

I'm sure that the person who created the concept of a college essay was a beady-eyed, sadistic, little hermit who only came out of his home to scare small children. And upon creation of the essay, he made all colleges put them on their applications or they would lose program accreditation. Sure, colleges will tell you that the essay helps them determine what kind of person you really are and gives them insight into your interests. Kind of makes you wonder about that interview a few months ago. Maybe they were just checking to see if you brushed your teeth.

I propose that instead of essays, prospective candidates make a video tape of their average day. Of course you then run into problems of staging and acting and then there's always some joker who will send in "Wild, Wild Cowgirls" or some other piece of cinematic excellence. This, however, could be remedied by leasing out Alan Funt and the rest of his crew. And then after editing, the board of admissions could gather round a big screen and watch "Candid Camera for Carleton College".

After all, kids have been writing for all of their lives and they'll have to write much more before they die. I'm not saying that the college essay is the root of all evils, and I know that my opinion is but one in a world of millions. But I stand resolved to find a better method for the college admissions process: one that will lead the teeming millions from the dark abyss of the essay and one that will also satisfy admissions directors across the nation while reducing the pain that we have endured for so long when our parents ask, "Have you written your essay yet?"

—JOHN LIBERSTEIN

COMMENT: Most admissions officers groan when they see yet another essay complaining about the essay. But if you have to write one—and what subject could be more compelling—John offers one that is lively.

*   *   *

Ever since I was little, I have heard a lot about business issues because my dad is a Professor of Finance at the University of Denver. There have been discussions on issues like bankruptcy, the stock market, management of money and banking. I had never thought too much about these discussions or business until my interest in business was sparked during high school.

There are many reasons why I am interested in business and feel that I am suited for the career. First, I have been very strong in math throughout my schooling. This year I am taking AP calculus and have a very high A in the class. I thoroughly enjoy working with numbers and money. Second, in business you have to be able to deal with people, and I feel I can do that. For three years I have worked at Mountain Music Academy as a secretary/receptionist. I am responsible for making phone calls to set up music lessons and I have to deal with people and their bills. From this experience, I learned how to deal with people and enjoy it. I like to work on a one-to-one basis with people, not closed up in a room by myself.

My interest in business, especially accounting, was sparked by my job at Mountain Music Academy. By my junior year, I had begun balancing books and working with taxes at the Academy. I loved it and became interested in accounting as a career. Then in my senior year, my interest was developed further by being Ad and Business Manager for the yearbook, and Treasurer of French Club and National Honor Society. Because of doing all these activities where I handle money and work with people, I feel I am capable of pursuing a career in business and find the idea exciting.

I do have interests in other academic areas besides business. I enjoy studying the English language and writing. I like the sciences, especially biology and I love history. However, I feel that I can do more with a business degree. I can work with people and go further than in the other academic areas. I enjoy working with numbers more than with microscopes or literature.

As far as education, I have always wanted to learn as much as I can and go as far as I can. So, in my plans, I would like to get an MBA and a Ph.D. I want to be as good as I possibly can be in my profession and will work for that. I want to be knowledgeable and capable enough to give people what they need. I feel that gaining more information from these extra years of education will give me the ability to aid others more and do the best possible job I can do. That's what's most important to me.

—ANGELA GILES

* * *

I remember my fifth-grade science teacher explaining to the class that the world is five billion years old. I remember my rabbi coming into the class (in retrospect, it seems to have been the very next hour) and saying that the world is five thousand years old.

At age nine, such problems did not bother me. I merely accepted the former when studying science and the latter during Bible class.

This early exposure to different and sometimes inconsistent ideas encouraged me to develop an open mind. I learned to evaluate new concepts without prejudgment and to apply them when appropriate without insisting that they represent absolute truth. I try to listen, learn, and evolve.

My studies in mathematics confirm my beliefs that one cannot accept any conclusion as indubitably proven. Every proof in mathematics and logic stems from unprovable axioms and postulates. This does not invalidate mathematics or logic. On the contrary, it gives them a greater degree of flexibility, of freedom. Mathematics becomes a tool with which we improve our understanding of the world around us. By applying different techniques, we can expand mathematics so that it encompasses physics, chemistry, economics, computer science, formal linguistics, and even psychology.

For example, non-Euclidean geometry differs from traditional high-school geometry in one postulate and, consequently, provides what may or may not be a more valid picture of the universe. My friends at our summer math program often became frustrated by the apparent contradictions with what they had previously learned. They repeatedly asked of the professor, "But which one is right—Euclidean or Lobachevskian geometry?"

This question did not bother me. I more readily accepted that the geometries are both self-consistent and logical and, therefore, they are both right. They are both true. Yet they are different.

My current studies in physics have further demonstrated

that prejudgement is fatal to the inquiring mind. A scientist who lacks an open mind is doomed to the mere imitation of old methods rather than the discovery of new ones. Scientific truths are not absolute and thus do not invalidate religious beliefs. Just as number systems are tools which help one understand the world, religion is a tool which helps an individual understand himself.

On Saturday mornings, I lead a junior high school youth group in my synagogue. In addition to Bible and Talmud, I teach them excerpts from *Kuzari*, a Jewish philosophical work. This book presents in a fairly unbiased manner the fundamentals of other religions and secular philosophies. The students are always interested to learn that their views are not universally accepted and that other opinions have an equal claim to validity. And only when one understands that his beliefs are not derivable by logic can he appreciate the significance of pure faith in his values.

However, there is a catch; a mind that recognizes the lack of absolute truths constantly needs new ideas to stimulate and improve itself. For this purpose, I cannot imagine a better place to spend the next four years of my life than Harvard University.

—David Cowan

COMMENT: Few college counselors would encourage a high school senior to write a short essay that deals with the relation of science and religion or absolute and relative truths. Yet there are many reasons that David's essay succeeds. His discussion is firmly grounded in personal experience, and he develops his argument with carefully selected evidence.

WRITING ABOUT EXTRA-CURRICULAR ACTIVITIES AND INTERESTS

John Thornburgh of Mountain Brook High in Birmingham, Alabama, now at Rice University, tells of understandings gained from his participation on the debating team, calling it his favorite "mental sport." Raymond Suke Flournoy from the San Diego Public School System, now at Harvard College, writes an essay that recounts his interest in speech competitions. His essay considers his motivations for participating in this particular extra-curricular activity. Matt Warren of the University of Illinois reflects upon his experiences in scouting and its help in defining his values. Tufts University's Andy Paster tells of traveling through Europe with his Scout troop. His essay illustrates a wide range of leadership responsibilities and their effect upon him. Carr McClain of Duke briefly tells of his main extra-curricular interest, animals. Crossroads School's Ted Epstein tells of his memories of performing before a less than receptive audience. Ted and his band are currently in New York City trying to break into the music business. Erik Dahms of the College of Wooster in Ohio relates the excitement of "living on the edge" in his '72 Oldsmobile Vista Cruiser. A Princeton student, Wendy Adams, draws an analogy between the high school juggling club that she founded and the juggling that she does with her own life. Debbie Feldacker, a student at the University of Chicago, discusses her lifetime goal of combining her three passions in life: people, dance, and the acquisition of knowledge. Debbie's essay tells of her involvement with S.A.D.D., teaching dance to youngsters, and the pleasures of intellectual debate. Involvement in drama is the subject of the next essay by

Yale's Carla Power. Carla's essay is followed by a Wisconsin student's views about the Model United Nations Program.

* * *

Of all the abilities that one may possess, perhaps the most important is the power to express one's ideas effectively so as to convince others of their value. In a free society, especially, the communication of ideas, on a large scale or small, plays a vital role in shaping the life of every individual. Accordingly, I believe that one of the most valuable activities available to students today is interscholastic debate, a mental "sport" in which teams compete to demonstrate superior organization, evidence, and persuasiveness. Personally, my experience with debate (which includes competition in nearly one hundred rounds, hours of preparation, and participation in summer forensics institutes) has had a significant impact on my development as a person—both intellectually and emotionally—for it has given me the opportunity not only to improve my skills of communication but also to learn to use those skills under pressure both in cooperation with my teammate and in competition with my opponents.

On an intellectual level, debate has helped me by requiring me to concentrate on thorough research techniques, rapid but valid analysis of ideas and arguments, clear organization, and, finally, effective, persuasive delivery of my thoughts to the judge. Of course, practice in these areas has indeed improved my debating. Very importantly, however, the skills refined by involvement with debate are hardly confined to being useful only for this one activity. Indeed, they are easily applied to all activities involving, for example, writing, and, in fact, they are actually vital to the success of virtually every scholar, businessman, professional, and leader. I thus can be certain that my efforts to excel at debate have truly had an important impact on my intellectual development.

Debate, however, has also been valuable to me on a more emotional level, for, in the real world, successful communication requires more than a particular technique. It also demands a certain amount of emotional preparation—preparation that includes the acceptance of two important facts: that effective communication is often only possible through the effort of multiple individuals, and that for every idea that one expresses there probably is a good counter-argument that one must be able to consider and discuss with grace. Debate, of course, has given me a greater understanding of each of these insights, the first because no debate is ever won or lost alone (without one's partner) and the second because almost every opposing team is able to introduce challenging new arguments that must be analyzed instantaneously without panic. Hence, I feel justified in saying that debate has played an important role in developing my emotional outlook toward key elements of life.

Overall, if the power to convince others of the value of one's ideas is indeed of the utmost importance (as it almost certainly is), then my efforts to succeed in debate must be described as far more than worthwhile. After all, throughout my life, I have been and will continue to be required to utilize the skills of debate to express my ideas both in speech and writing—when taking exams, interacting with friends, working in my profession, and attempting to improve the society of which I am a part—and, of course, the degree of skill that I exhibit when participating in these activities will have a profound influence not only on my life but also on the lives of many others.

—JOHN THORNBURGH

COMMENT: Example of a very clear, well-organized, but impersonal essay.

*   *   *

While preparing my application for Harvard University, I asked one of my former math teachers if he would write a recommendation for me. He readily agreed, but requested that he might first ask me a few questions in order that the recommendation be more comprehensive and complete. In the course of that brief interview, he asked me about numerous aspects of myself, including my upbringing, education, and goals in life. I found one set of questions particularly thought-provoking. "What is your motivation?" he asked. "Why do you try so hard in school, and if you did not earn the honors and awards, would you still try as hard?" I had to laugh, because in that last statement, he had described quite accurately my involvement in speech competitions. The scenario of my being left "honorless" is truer than he might have thought.

It is a fact, that I have earned a fair number of awards during my secondary school years, not only for academics, but for involvement in mathematics, history, art, and fencing competitions. For speech, though, I have not received such immediate rewards.

I first became involved with speech competition in May when I placed second in a field of five in a very small oratory round. Encouraged by this, I soon became very active on my school's speech team. I attended the regular meetings, wrote, memorized, and practiced numerous speeches, and competed after school and on the weekends in large speech tournaments. Yet, for all that work, time, and energy, I never reached a finals round again. After each competition, I would practice harder, rewrite my speeches, and change my delivery, doing my best to prepare for the next tournament. The best I ever did was to miss making finals by only one point.

Why then did I continue to be involved with speech? Why not turn my attentions to a pastime more appreciative of my efforts? The truth is, because I enjoy competing in speech. I enjoy the fun and challenge of it. I enjoy meeting new people and being involved in my school's activities. Of course, winning is nice, but garnering an award or accolade never was and never will be my primary objective. My motivation goes much deeper than that. During my years in school, I have realized that if I can truthfully state that I have done my best, then that is enough. This is what I told my former math teacher. No one has to be constantly tempting me with rewards for me to do well. What I do, I choose to do, and when I do work at something, I only hope to do the best that I possibly can. I cannot ask any more, but if I give any less, all of the honors and awards in the world will not help.

— RAYMOND SUKE FLOURNOY

COMMENT: Perhaps only someone who wins a lot of honors can have the luxury of writing about an activity in which he isn't a winner. And perhaps that is what makes Raymond's claims that he competes in speech for sheer enjoyment ring true. Raymond also has sufficient self-confidence to use an arresting opening that at first does not seem complimentary to him.

* * *

A question circled the campfire as an eager eleven-year-old contemplated his answer.

"Matt, what is your goal in Scouting?" came the voice from across the flames.

"I want to make Eagle," I solemnly replied, being full of self-confidence. I knew very little of the goal for which I was striving, or of the tribulations which I would have to endure.

Well, I "made Eagle" and by virtue of that fact I am now a dandy fellow and outstanding citizen.

No!

The reason I chose to write about Scouting is one of definition. My Scouting experiences have given me greater self-knowledge and an early realization of just what I value in life.

The early years of my career were, in simplest terms, a lot of fun. I received a tremendous thrill working with and for nature with other guys who had the same feelings. There was an atmosphere of strong motivation to learn and accomplish. Merit badges and skill awards were garnered with ease. I faced my fear of snakes, which I "knew" were waiting for me to fall asleep before they struck at me from the slimy recesses of the tent. Having to go without Mom and Dad for a whole week, I learned to cook and clean for myself and others. Responsibility emerged, and although I sometimes failed, I truly tried to do well in all of my endeavors from rock rappelling to boiling some atrocious Mulligan Stew. My work culminated at the Court of Honor. The Court provided recognition of my deeds, and I received a sense of accomplishment from the award, whether it was a Safety merit badge or attaining the rank of Star.

Eighth grade began a time of inner turmoil for me. Scouting was not "cool." Parents were always fascinated and impressed with a "nice" young man who did community service work. But, a fourteen-year-old girl was certainly not to be wooed with:

"Hey baby, I just got my Mammals merit badge! Wanna dance?"

This, of course, is a fictitious extreme, but it nevertheless points out the dilemma I faced. My peers had decided that the Boy Scouts was not an organization for a teenager in the eighties to be a part of, and I foolishly began to believe them.

Scouting became a chore. I dreaded Wednesdays because that meant I had a meeting. Under no circumstances was the uniform to be worn in public, or was Scouting to be discussed outside of the Troop. If issues demanded discussion in public places, the cynical initials "B.S." were used. To compound all of this "shame," the vice of procrastination had slowed my advancement toward my goal of Eagle. I was truly feeling distressed. What had once given me great pleasure was not something I loathed. Although I was not very far from Eagle, I seriously thought of quitting—ending this "burden."

One day my thoughts drifted back to my campfire. I remembered my goal and I remembered what I had received from Scouting. I ran the evidence through my head over and over in an attempt to make the right decision. The most mature realization of my life dawned upon me during my search for an answer. If I were to quit for the sake of conformity, not only would I have wasted my efforts, but I would have lost my identity. I envisioned myself at the age of forty asking, "What if I had only stuck in and completed my Eagle?" Anger directed at *myself*, from *myself* for the rest of *my* life was a scary prospect. I went on to "make Eagle" knowing that I would always be proud of the honor and of my decision to persevere.

—MATT WARREN

COMMENT: Matt's amused memories of himself and his contemplation of the problems of conformity give a fresh look at becoming an Eagle Scout. His realistic appraisal of the real benefits and costs of continuing in the Scouts convinces us more than all the familiar glowing platitudes would.

*   *   *

One evening while I was camping along the banks of the Green River in Utah with a group from a summer camp, a flash flood swept through our campsite, carrying with it our rafts, food, and other equipment, leaving only some personal gear and a little water. With the help of another group and their canoes, we swam and paddled nineteen miles down the river until we found one of our rafts. We then made a second trip down the river to pick up the gear we had left behind. Although I joined Scouting because I liked camping and the outdoors, it was this experience that made me appreciate how much I had learned from Scouting. Not only had I acquired camping and survival skills but more importantly, I was able to provide instruction and leadership. Throughout the entire situation, I felt that I knew what to do and I was confident that I could accomplish the task. This awareness greatly strengthened my commitment to become an Eagle Scout.

My quest for the goal of Eagle, which is most meaningful to me, has been a long and difficult one over the past six years, with each new challenge adding a greater meaning and importance to the goal. As I have met the challenge of the multitude of progressive levels, I have found that there are always higher goals for which to strive. Through my experiences I have learned a great deal about myself and others.

One of my most memorable Scouting activities was my trip to Europe. During the trip I held the position of Senior Patrol Leader. Since I was in charge of twelve other scouts, I used the opportunity to further develop my leadership skills. It was quite a challenge to take care of everyone's needs and to keep the group together in the busy streets. The trip lasted two weeks and took us through nine countries. It was extremely educational and inspiring to meet scouts and other people from all over the world and to learn about many different places and cultures. On the other hand, I was fascinated by basic similarities between our ways of life and realized how slight the differences between people really are.

Of the many different cities of the eleven countries in which I have participated in Scouting activities, the most striking city was Luzern, Switzerland, founded in the early 1300's. I was impressed by the modern style youth hostel there. The contrast in architecture showed the ability of the city to mix the old with the new, to achieve a functional yet beautiful balance.

Although the different languages of Europe were a slight problem, our ability to overcome the language barrier was best exemplified during a soccer game with other visitors at the youth hostel in Luxemburg. Though no one spoke the other's language, we managed to communicate through our mutual desire.

Such experiences illustrate how I have been influenced by a wide range of scouting activities. I now hold the highest troop position possible for a person under eighteen and when I am old enough, I plan to become an Assistant Scoutmaster and maybe later on a Scoutmaster, so that I can stay close to the Scouting program. As I have continued to be involved in Scouting, I have found, especially when working with other younger and less knowledgable Scouts, that the benefits and rewards of Scouting are countless and that the greater my investment into the program, the greater the rewards. It is my desire that through my leadership positions in the troop and elsewhere I will be able to pass on to younger Scouts the knowledge and enjoyment that I have received from Scouting and that I can apply my knowledge and experience to all of my future endeavors.

—ANDY PASTER

COMMENT: The drama of the opening leads the reader into Andy's more predictable account of Scouting experiences.

* * *

Throughout my life animals have been my main nonacademic interest. I became fascinated with dinosaurs at a very young age, and my interest was reinforced by my family's frequent trips to the Smithsonian Institute in Washington, where I spent hours in the Museum of Natural History. My interest in dinosaurs quickly expanded to include all animals, and I had the privilege of seeing the National Zoo in Washington several times and of taking one special trip to the Bronx Zoo in New York. For two summers I held a job at our small, local Mill Mountain Zoo and enjoyed being close to the animals on a daily basis and observing their care.

I have read extensively about animals, and ever since childhood, have been collecting a beautiful library on the subject. My books range from heavily illustrated overviews of the breadth of the animal kingdom to highly technical ones on but a handful of species.

An unusual aspect of my love of animals is my love of hunting. I imagine that many people would find it difficult both to enjoy seeing live animals in a zoo and to kill them in their natural environments. My hunting hobby is family-inspired because my father grew up in a rural valley where hunting and fishing were the only available forms of recreation. I began hunting with my father as a child, and now the highlight of my time in the woods with him each year is a week-long deer hunt at Thanksgiving.

I have been able to be both a hunter and lover of animals because I recognize the ecological necessity of the sport in the eastern United States. Man has virtually eliminated most of our nation's natural predators, permitting America's herbivores, such as deer and moose, to proliferate unchecked. If no controls are put upon the populations of these animals, they will outstrip their food supplies. An example of lethal overpopulation occurred recently among deer living in the Everglades. Rabid environmentalists thwarted a mercy-kill of the Florida animals, resulting in the starvation and death of a vast number of them. Controlled hunting results in the deaths of a small number of animals so that the majority may forage and live healthy lives. The sport is honorable and time-honored, and a knowledgable animal-lover can enjoy it.

—CARR MCCLAIN

COMMENT: Carr shows he knows what he is talking about by being specific, and he shows he has thought about the apparent contradiction of being an animal lover and a hunter. The short essay reveals him knowledgeable and thoughtful.

*   *   *

I was jolted out of bed around 5:00 on Saturday afternoon with the realization that I had overslept. I suppose my body was demanding compensation for that day's mid-morning rehearsal and the late rehearsal the night before. I hopped in and out of the shower and dressed in the clothes I had meticulously laid out for the evening.

The phone rang just as I was struggling with the buttons on my shirt sleeve. Andy and I each recognized the other's voice, so we skipped the usual decorum of asking and greeting. The phone conversation took 5 seconds or less. "Ted? What's going o-"

"Just yell at me later; I overslept and I'm on my way." I finished dressing, said a quick goodbye to my mother—who wished me luck—and drove to the factory.

"The factory" refers to the vacant office area in my father's electric heater manufacturing plant where we were allowed to practice: me on my drumset (the reward for two summers spent working at the factory), Andy on his guitar and a loaned amplifier (because his own had a blown fuse), and Gabe on his bass which he played through an amp the size (and nearly the weight) of a refrigerator, and which seemed to sound different each time we practiced. The factory was where it all took place; all of the personal battles, the interpersonal battles, the battles against time, money, inertia, despair, and always the worst of circumstances. All of this we overcame for the rewards we got, or felt that we had the potential to get.

We loved music, Andy's original compositions. We understood, in spite of the fact that our high-powered instrumentals weren't the most marketable music around, that they were some of the best. We respected each other's musicianship, each other's creativity, and our ability as individuals and as a band to come up with interesting, powerful, and original musical ideas. And we had been proceeding, slowly but with determination, to get the recognition that we knew we deserved.

When I arrived at the factory that day, Gabe and Andy already had started packing up my drums. After we had loaded the equipment, including Gabe's refrigerator, into our parents' cars, we were on our way. We didn't, however, quite know the nature of the place to which we were going. When we arrived at the Smith's Tavern in a quiet corner of north St. Louis, we could tell from the outside that the place was seedy. Still, we didn't have any notion of what we would find inside, and it didn't expect us, either.

When I walked through the screen door and into the tavern, I spent a few seconds just taking it all in. The average age in the bar must have been about 55. Customers sat around, chatting happily and bobbing their heads to the Kenny Rogers tune that was blaring quietly from what sounded like a two-inch speaker in the jukebox. I inconspicuously brought an arm load of drums back to the dimly lit area where I saw the guitarist from another local band tuning up amidst a mishmash of equipment which the other bands had brought. The first thing I heard when I walked back outside was Andy saying that he "couldn't have imagined a more profound juxtaposition in a nightmare."

Before the first band went on, an obese man in a tank-top, jeans, and a bushy beard approached the guitarist and said, "I know y'all don't know any country 'n' western, but can you play any Bob Seeger or Foreigner or anything like 'at?" We knew we were in trouble. While the first band played their set, we prayed that some people would arrive who would come with the intention of watching the bands. I don't think we would have lasted long playing for the regular Smith's Tavern clientele. Luckily, some listeners did show up, so we had a barrier of twenty-or-so between ourselves and the regular customers. No one danced, but that was all right. Just listening to and enjoying our music seems appropriate.

About halfway through the set, we received some complaints from the customers, but we ignored them in favor of the applause we heard from those who had come to see the show. But they too had a complaint: they couldn't hear the drums. I wasn't aware of this until after the show, since I was situated behind the guitar amplifiers. My carefully planned and practiced parts had come across as a lot of impressive flailing. But we had our impact anyway. That's all we really wanted. It didn't matter that a woman from one of the tables would rather have heard "some Huey Lewis and the News," it didn't matter that only a handful of people listened to us, it didn't matter to any great extent that the loaned amplifier Andy was using made his playing sound like a 747 landing in a minor key, and it didn't even matter that I walked out only 6 dollars richer than I was when I walked in. We had put on a good show, we had shown people that we were something special, we had made an impact. That was the greatest reward.

—TED EPSTEIN

COMMENT: It's a good story, but what does it show a college about Ted? Plenty! In addition to his ability to tell a good story, Ted shows the admissions officers that he is an excellent, sensitive observer; that he is involved and experienced in music; that he can face difficult situations. And it doesn't hurt to keep the reader interested!

*   *   *

As I was driving down the Parkway, I had second thoughts (lots of them) and almost went straight home, but I thought "wow! living on the edge!" and kept going. Depending on your point of view, you may or may not view driving a '72 Oldsmobile Vista Cruiser station wagon without a license as dangerous. I did. Part of my motivation was this concept of "dangerous fun" which caused me to completely abandon my values and ethics for the sole purpose of attending a party. However, none of my second thoughts managed to stay me from driving on.

When I reached the neighborhood where this social event of the year was taking place, I realized that I really had no idea where it was and promptly got lost. I thought about driving home and forgetting the whole thing, but an impulsive and foolish thought entered into my mind. This thought was "wow! what a story this will make!" Now my adrenaline was really pumping as I was contemplating and imagining the manner in which my exploits would be glorified on Monday morning.

But, as I was making a u-turn, fate intervened and the car stalled right in the middle of a street, completely blocking it. After about 10 minutes of utterly futile attempts to start the car, the long arm of the law reached out in the form of a neighborhood guard (who has no real powers of arrest and is frequently addressed by the "trendy" set as a rent-a-cop). Uh oh. What if he asks me for my driver's license? Now I had to think up a reasonably plausible story/fabrication/fib/lie to tell this man if he asked to see my driver's license. The first question out of his mouth was, "Do you have a driver's license, son?" The only one that I couldn't honestly answer yes. I tried hard to stall while I was thinking of how I could convince him that I *really* did have a license, but somehow couldn't locate it before I left the house. However, while my mind was trying to make up something, my mouth said "no".

Shortly thereafter, a real policeman arrived on the scene, verified the facts, wrote me a ticket and court summons and then proceeded to try to find someone to jump-start the car and drive it home (legally). I found the party and asked two friends for their help. After a search for jumper cables, we had an uneventful ride home. I got out of the car, thanked Kent and Devonne and turned around to see my mother and father pull up. "Hold it right there, young man!" After I explained that Kent and Devonne had done nothing other than drive me home, and my father told me in no uncertain terms his opinion of my actions of late, my parents and I had a long discussion. Earlier in the evening, had I been asked, I would have stated my motivation for this escapade to be something along the lines of "dangerous fun". But, once subjected to greater scrutiny, even the concept of "dangerous fun" has its roots in something else . . . peer pressure. It may or may not seem incredible to you that peer pressure could cause someone to go joyriding in their parent's car, but that was my only real motivation. Because of this incident, I am much more aware of this problem, and this awareness helps me make much more prudent decisions regarding school and my social life.

The ticket and court summons were resolved when the judge threw the case out because the police officer never saw me actually driving the car. I had to pay $14 in court costs. Looking back, I realized that if I had thought quickly and lied, I might have gone home scot-free. But, I think that it was better that I was truthful, even though a lie would have saved me a lot of fear and anxiety in the short term. Overall, this experience helped me realize some of my strengths and shortcomings, taught me a lesson about peer pressure and, . . . I have not stolen any cars since.

—ERIK DAHMS

COMMENT: After all those essays about how good the writers are, admissions readers must be relieved to come across Erik's account of joyriding without a license. The ending of the essay, in which Erik shows how he has learned from the experience, should quiet the admissions committee's fears about letting him on campus.

*   *   *

When several friends and I founded the first Juggling Club in our school last year, the "sport" became one of my favorite activities. The goal of the hobby, trying to keep several objects in the air at one time struck me as analogous to what I've been trying to do in my life: be an active member of society both by participating in many and varied activities and interests and by trying to get other people, all very different from each other, to do the same.

When you learn to juggle, you start with a single tennis ball or beanbag, tossing and catching it with one hand, making sure you get the fundamental motion down pat before moving on. When I started high school, that first basic factor was, of course, academics. Older friends had warned me that the amount of work increased geometrically when you got to "real" school, and I was duly cautious. I spent the first few weeks making sure I had a grip on all my classes before deciding I could venture into other areas.

Activities and social life, naturally, were and are vital interests, and they became the second "ball" that I wanted to be able to suspend. The second step in actual juggling is with two balls in one hand, keeping them rotating in a circle and thereby sustaining them both. This takes a bit of practice, both literally and figuratively, but it is the most fundamental balance of two things to try to achieve in high school. I am still working on making room for the paper, clubs, and get-togethers with friends while leaving sufficient time for reading and research.

The aforementioned friends are a juggling challenge in themselves. I enjoy myself and feel equally at home with three groups of friends, who, if they must be categorized, would be the pseudo-intellects, who have long conversations where we solve all the world's problems; the social people, who get together at open parties, dances, and such; and the simple-pleasures people, among whom are my closest friends, who would rather congregate at my house and watch *Monty Python and the Holy Grail* for the nineteenth time than go out and wait to be entertained. I'm not schizophrenic; I truly enjoy the company of all these people, they all have much in the way of friendship to offer me, and I try to balance them with equal attention.

Once you have attained juggling three balls, you have achieved the main goal, and it is fine being satisfied with that. Recently, however, I felt there was a lack somewhere and that I needed something more. I tried adding another major interest, that of religion, and now it is a renewed challenge to try to balance academics, extracurricular activities, and a variety of friends, and simultaneously be striving for a fulfilling relationship with God.

I will have worked for three years in high school trying to achieve a good balance of all my interests, and when I go on to college, I will have to start all over with the same goal, gradually working my way up to the desired number of "balls." I hope my foundations in doing so will make college a profitable and beneficial experience.

—WENDY ADAMS

COMMENT: Wendy's organizational device—the analogy between the juggling club and her life—provides novelty, but novelty justified by content.

*   *   *

I do not have a "career objective" or an "academic objective," but rather, I have a lifetime goal. My lifetime goal is to combine my three greatest passions in life: people, dance and the acquisition of knowledge. High school has been a stepping stone in accomplishing this combination and college will be another step towards personal fulfillment.

My love of people is expressed through community service and a part-time job. I am the co-president and founder of the first S.A.D.D. (Students Against Driving Drunk) chapter at my school. I devote much time to it because I believe youth is the future and we should not allow the needless teen-age deaths that can be prevented through the workings of the S.A.D.D.

program. In the past two years a growing awareness and concern for each other's safety has developed at Clayton, and I hope it will continue. In addition to work at Clayton High School, I speak for S.A.D.D. in my community. Once a month I speak at the Juvenile Detention Center about the importance of stopping drunk driving. Many people do not believe these juvenile offenders are worthwhile, but I realize that they are in the same age category and are subject to the same pressures that I face. I believe they value the time I spend with them. I, too, value this time because I gain a different perspective on life. I look forward to my monthly meetings with these young people. Often, we just talk about life as a teenager, because many of them have no one else with whom to converse and vent their feelings.

Aside from S.A.D.D., I am in a performing dance group. We perform twice a year at nursing homes or senior citizens' apartments. We know how much the residents truly appreciate the youth and excitement that we bring to them because of their applause and endless smiles. Their outward appreciation is comparatively less to the inward rewards I feel when I dance for them. I am very proud to be part of a group that recognizes the warmth associated with community service.

My part-time job is teaching dance to young children. I work seven hours a week teaching about 80 students. They too perform for others, and truly enjoy it. I bring an enthusiasm to my work and exert a lot of energy to make dance fun for them. The most exciting part of my job, in contrast to my friends working at McDonald's, is that my work has a lasting influence. My students learn coordination and skills that they would not otherwise have learned. I find satisfaction in seeing the self-confidence they feel. My job has been a most rewarding part of high school. I hope I can continue these types of community service throughout my life.

For me, dance is an outlet for personal expression. I have danced approximately eight hours per week throughout high school. Dance has given me a goal of perfection. I work very intensely, not for my teacher, not for my audience, but for myself. My dancing has given me uniqueness among my peers and has enhanced an "artsy" side to my family. I have been with two St. Louis ballet companies and have performed at least forty times in the St. Louis area. I have gained self-confidence, strength and a sense of freedom to express myself through movement. I love performing. I love seeing people smile and their happiness makes me exert more energy and work harder. My love for dance extends into love for theatre and music. Though my personal abilities are not as strong in either, I enjoy being part of the beauty and excitement of both. I hope I can enhance my enjoyment of performing arts by being active in them at college and incorporating them into my career.

The acquisition of knowledge has been an integral part of my high school career. I have attended a leadership conference for drug abuse prevention, been active in a youth group, and twice attended a summer school purely for the pleasure of intellectual stimulation. At the leadership conference, I was stimulated by an atmosphere of people vehemently trying to learn from each other ways to eliminate drug abuse and counsel its victims. With the youth group, I discussed the abstractions of God, afterlife, and religious theory. During summer school, I took a class in legal systems where we discussed such issues as effective punishment, the current justice system, and ways to improve morality. I also took a course in journalism where I toured St. Louis with selected high schoolers from various districts, discovered hidden treasures in my own city, and wrote about them. All of these adventures were rewarding for me because I learned ideas, exchanged thoughts and gained knowledge in creative settings. My advanced English class at school analyzes the philosophies of Plato and Aristotle. We enter into heated discussions about the equality of Man or the "reason for poetry". The entire class is a peripatetic journey. It is this creative and valuable knowledge that I treasure, the knowledge that comes from discussion and discovery. I hope college can further this quest for ideas, and I hope my career will enable me to be creative with my work, thus utilizing the knowledge I will acquire.

My lifetime goal is to find the career that will combine my interests but still allow me to grow. I believe that being in public or community relations, a children's talent coordinator or casting director, a manager of a dance academy, or a choreographer could fulfill my career desires. However, I am sure that I can and will discover many more possibilities during the course of my college career.

—DEBBIE FELDACKER

* * *

Drama remains my most useful artistic experience, for it emphasizes the individual, be it me as an actress, or the character I portray. It seems the most humanistic of the humanities, for drama involves one human interpreting another—the character.

Oscar Wilde once said that not going to the theater was like "preparing one's toilet without a mirror." Wilde's image describes my feelings toward seeing plays, but more specifically, toward acting in them. Acting has served me as a mirror for reflecting both myself and others. I have acted for most of my life—in school plays, scene study classes and workshops, and playreadings. Thus far, I have approached roles in two different ways. Characters that I identify with strongly, such as Anne Frank, I use as a medium for direct self-expression. The role becomes much like a slide projector through which I can project myself. This method, requiring introspection, is a convenient conveyance for me, for, like most adolescents, I spend hours in self-analysis, trying to untangle emotions and to explore my reactions to the outside world. The self-absorption required in an actor may well be the cause of so many adolescents becoming "stage-struck." In playing a role, I often use the same techniques I use in trying to mature. In other roles, however, acting requires maturity, sensitivity to others, and observation. When I played Rita in *Educating Rita* or Big Nurse in *One Flew Over the Cuckoo's Nest*, I had to repress my own character, and create a new one. When I played Rita, I collected characteristics from eclectic sources: the accent from a London shopgirl, and the ingenuousness from one of my mother's night school students. For Big Nurse, I imagined Orwell's Big Brother crossed with a well-oiled reaping machine. This second acting "process" requires knowledge of others, rather than of oneself.

Drama centers on the actor knowing himself and others. From it, I have learned about people, the root of all the arts and humanities.

—CARLA POWER

COMMENT: Carla goes beyond the expected response here to show the complexity of her thought about acting. Specific references to roles she's had also remind the reader of the extent of her dramatic experience.

*   *   *

I have been active in Model United Nations for four years, a member of the area-wide Steering Committee for two, and plan to continue my participation at college. Model U.N. appeals to me because it is an excellent forum for debate and the exchange of ideas. It allows me to improve my public speaking skills while discussing pertinent world issues. Politics is an avocation for me, and Model U.N. provides an opportunity for my opinions to be heard. By discussing world problems with informed, dedicated delegates, I gain a greater perspective on both the topic and the validity of my arguments. For these reasons, along with the sheer fun of the sessions, I hope to be an active participant in the National Model U.N.

—ANONYMOUS

WRITING ABOUT ATHLETIC EXPERIENCES

The examples that follow show that interesting sports experiences can make fine essays. Jason Barton of Lawrence University records his dedication to soccer as a player and fan. The University of Maine's Jeff Gold speaks of his love for a variety of sports, in particular ice hockey. David Pokorny of Northwestern University writes of the inspiration of a rival runner. His essay stresses a personal sense of contentment in modest achievement.

* * *

There was a light fog hovering what seemed like inches above my head as I got off at the New Cross Gate tube stop in southeast London. I was told by a bobby, perched up against a board displaying arrival and departure times, that I had about a ten-minute walk to my destination. Trying to follow the directions closely, I turned onto several sidestreets, past rows of typical British houses, brick two-stories with shutters, and small, neatly manicured lawns. And then I was there, "The Den," the small stadium that was home to the Milwall Football Club. A great longing of mine, to be witness to a European soccer game, was about to be fulfilled.

My passion for soccer, however, is not exclusively restricted to a place in the stands. From the first time I kicked a soccer ball at the age of ten, I knew I was on to something great. One of the greatest achievements of my high school career was making the Varsity team as a sophomore. Against sometimes sarcastic criticism from my peers, who told me I didn't have what it took to play competitive soccer, I was one of four sophomores who made the Varsity team out of a pool of twenty or so of my classmates. Still there were those who said that my making the team was a fluke, and that the coach would come to his senses next year. But it was such a feeling of exhilaration to make the team and prove to myself that I had what it took.

With this personal victory, I learned I also had to suffer defeat. With my level of self-esteem at full throttle from the year before, I returned from my summer vacation in England ready to do it again. But on the very first day of tryouts I severely sprained my ankle. Eventually it healed but during the rest of tryouts I never played to my full potential. When the time came around for cuts to be made, my coach approached me and informed me that I wasn't giving it all I had, and that the team had no place for players who didn't give it their all. I tried to reason with him, explaining my fear of re-injuring my ankle, but to no avail. I was not to be a member of the Varsity soccer team during my junior year. Embarrassed, humiliated and most of all bitter, I stormed off. The worst part of not making the team was not that I wouldn't be there, but that it seemed to justify others' sentiments that I should never have made the team in the first place. I tried the best I could to deal with my resentment and anger, but they never left me completely.

Even through my defeat, my passion for the game was not lessened. I still appreciated it for what it was, the universal language. It is not only far and away the most popular sport in the world, crossing over political boundaries and uniting people of all nationalities with one common link; it is also, I think, the most graceful, fluid and flowing form of sport known to man. And unlike football or basketball, where size is the most important qualification, soccer mainly requires intelligence, or field vision. The ability to perceive everything on the field at once, to be able to watch one thing while peripherally watching another, intuitively knowing, meanwhile, what is going on behind you—that is field vision.

Sometimes at school I want to argue with those who try to tell me how football is better than soccer. I feel like going up to the quarterback and shaking him and saying, "Don't you see, are you that naive?" Ah, well, anyone who has seen soccer played knows its true beauty—the continual flow of the game, of bodies in motion, fluid, natural rhythm. Football, on the other hand, with its clash of pad on pad, its bone-shattering tackles is akin to only one thing: out and out war. But I know I'll never go up to the quarterback and say those things, because attacking football at our school is like spitting on the flag.

Admittedly, with a large chip on my shoulder and something to prove not only to myself, but to my peers, the coaches and my school, I went out for Varsity soccer this year, my last year of high school. I made it.

—JASON BARTON

COMMENT: The opening is atmospheric; the body of the essay clearly shows Jason's tremendous loyalty to the sport of soccer. Do the opening and the body go together?

*   *   *

On an early Sunday morning in September the air of the arena was quite cool yet I was practically sweating with nervousness. The hockey tryouts are always intense—each player is numbered for observation as he skates through fundamental drills. The observers were for the most part gray-haired coaches with stoic faces, steaming coffee, and enormous clip boards. Their pens were moving almost as fast as my heart was beating. After every player had gone through the drills there was a scrimmage that lasted for the remainder of the session.

As it turned out I got the starting position at center, not because of outstanding skills but, I was told, because of the "aggressive hustle" I displayed. This tryout was for a midget open level team and since then, I have been noticed by other junior teams in addition to the varsity high school team I now play for. Because of the small size of my school we do not have a hockey team. However, Generic High School has had a team but for the past two years has had trouble filling the roster. I was noticed by an assistant coach of the Generic team and was given the opportunity to play after a successful tryout.

Besides ice hockey, I enjoy other sports that complement my level of play on the ice. Since the eighth grade, I have become a serious soccer player and have many memorable moments because of it. I am also an avid bicyclist and have been on many bicycle tours including two over two-hundred miles. Hoping to refine my skills and knowledge of hockey, I attended Huron Hockey School in Ontario, Canada, last summer and plan to make a return visit this summer as well.

Participation in sports, especially ice hockey, has been a tremendous source of competition and cooperation for me, two motivating aspects that have helped balance my growth as an adolescent. My respect for teammates, classmates, work associates, and friends has given me these aspects, and with the help of a sometimes overwhelming superego, I strive for concrete achievement . . .

My exposure to different people and my participation in activities, such as student government and ice hockey, have provided me with the experience of competition and cooperation, aspects of life on which I thrive. Since junior high school these activities have helped me immensely in my growth as an adolescent. As an athlete I have developed self-esteem and received gratifying recognition. However, as a worker and a student in different social environments, I have grown in a more important way by capturing a better understanding of life and my place in it.

—JEFF GOLD

COMMENT: The opening paragraph displays Jeff's acute observations; the last paragraph state some generalizations. Do these two paragraphs seem to be part of the same essay? If you had to send only one paragraph on to a college, which would you choose?

*   *   *

Sometimes the people whom we meet merely in passing have more influence and impact on life than those people who have been lifelong friends. I was fortunate enough to make such an acquaintance through my experiences as a runner. The person who has had the greatest impact on my personality is not my coach or a former team member, but a competitor from another school. Although I have never been with him for more than thirty minutes and always in a competitive setting, he has significantly influenced my views on competition, the strength of the group over the individual, and self satisfaction in achievement.

I first learned Scott Smith's name at Cross Country district competition my junior year. He began the race strongly, in second place, yet throughout the race I expected to see him dropping position, overstrained and exhausted. He didn't run out of drive and finished in fourth place, easily qualifying for the state meet (the top ten individuals qualify), while I strained for the finish in ninth place. At that point I decided that he was a better runner than I and he would continue outrunning me in track in the spring. My assumption proved false.

The next time I remember running against Scott was in the Track Sectionals, the final competition for State qualification. We were competing in the two mile run with six other runners; the top four finishers would qualify for the state meet. The sky had been overcast during the day, yet a quarter hour before the starting gun sent us down the track, the sun burned through the clouds heating up the cinder track and the air above it. The race was the most competitive and grueling two miles which I have ever run. The first and last runners were never separated by more than six yards and the maneuvering was so close that

I was spiked twice, although I didn't realize it until after the finish. The race remained close until the eighth and final lap. I was running in fifth place and Scott was in fourth when he suddenly moved to the outside, leaving just enough space on the inside of the track for me to move up. When I did he began yelling, yet what was most curious was that he was yelling "Go Clayton!! Get out of here! Get moving!!" I had just taken over his position, the final spot to qualify for State, and he still found enough energy and sportsmanship to help me run faster. I passed another runner and finished in third; Scott finished in fifth failing to qualify for State. I ran a warmdown lap with him and, still in shock, asked him why he did such a crazy and unselfish thing. His reply was simply, "I thought you had a better chance to qualify."

At that moment I became an instant supporter of Scott Smith. At every race thereafter I hollered for him on the sidelines and always wished him luck before our races against each other. I had put it out of mind that he would ever do anything so generous again. I was wrong.

The 1984 Cross Country season had gone well, yet I doubted that I would win the district because another especially strong runner, Jim Todd, was in my district. Jim's times were minutes ahead of mine so I went into districts expecting to finish second or third; luckily Scott was also in my district. I had been behind Jim for the majority of the three mile race and I was running neck and neck with Scott, our voices silent. As we approached the two mile mark, a steep hill, it seemed that Jim would easily win, because his lead had stretched to 150 yards, yet Scott thought otherwise. When we reached the base of the relentless slope Scott turned to me and shouted, "Look up the hill! Look up, come on drive your legs! Come on, DRIVE 'EM!!" Together we scrambled up the hill and as we reached the crest he pushed me on, saying, "Let's go, you can get him! Come on, go get that Neff!!" I returned coaxing, "You're coming with me, LET'S GO!!" Running side by side, we picked up the distance. I passed Jim Todd strongly and built up a commanding lead, while Scott chose to run with Todd, trying to beat him in the sprint. I eventually won the meet but before I celebrated I returned to the finish line to inspire Scott in his final sprint against Todd. When he did beat Neff, my celebration was twice as jubilant, for not only had I achieved, I had also been part of another person's achievement.

I owe much of my thrill in competition to Scott. He showed me that there is a time to realize when one cannot physically compete any longer. He showed me that competitors are not necessarily competing against each other as much as they are competing against their own limits. With his help I've realized that there are many things which cannot be achieved alone, but "with a little help from my friends," one can achieve the universe. Most important, though, he introduced me to contentment in modest achievement, without which one goes through life dissatisfied and dejected.

—DAVID POKORNY

COMMENT: David's essay combines the suspense of narratives of races with a discussion of these races' significance for him. David's tributes to his competitor ring true because he has grounded them in the specific reality of the exciting track meets.

WRITING ABOUT EMOTIONAL EXPERI-ENCES

In the following essays students share disappointing, dramatic, or painful personal experiences. Carr McClain, from the North Cross School in Roanoke and now at Duke, tells of the aftermath of the death of a beloved sister. Lydia Magliozzi of Harvard College writes about her reaction to an act of gratuitous violence. Matthew DeGreeff, also from Harvard, tells of the resolve born of being excluded from an Honors English program. A student at Miami University of Ohio, Matt Koster, writes of his reaction to his parents' divorce, drawing conclusions concerning the nature of the acceptance of pain.

* * *

I cannot choose one happening as the most significant in my emotional and intellectual development because of two extraordinary events during the recent years of my life. I want to tell you about them both.

On March 9, 1982, my sister Erin, my only sibling, was killed in a terrible automobile accident. She was on her way to a piano lesson at the North Carolina School of the Arts with our mother when they were struck head-on by a car traveling in the wrong direction. I lost a sister who was brilliant and kind and adored me. Following the wreck I had to cope with the shock Erin's absence and my mother's long hospitalization and recuperation. I faced the difficult task of helping my father and grandmother run a household and was charged with driving a carpool only a week after receiving my license.

My greatest challenge during this tragic time was maintaining my grades and class standing. In addition to added responsibilities outside of school, I played on the frequently-traveling North Cross golf team and had to miss many classes. That spring I learned the survival skills, independence, and determination that are essential to success at a powerful university. While our family tragedy has toughened me emotionally for the rigors of college existence, my days last summer at the Virginia Governor's School for the Gifted gave me a glimpse of the exciting possibilities of undergraduate intellectual life. I spent four weeks at Virginia Polytechnic Institute with two hundred and three of the brightest minds in our state. We lived in a dormitory, took courses from university professors, and had access to many of Virginia Tech's vast resources. The students at Governor's School were, beyond being bright, Virginia's most enthusiastic learners. No grades were given for achievement; we competed only with ourselves, motivated by interest instead of necessity. Governor's School stirred in me a new eagerness for study that will spur me to investigate the resources of a richly endowed university such as Duke.

The courses the professors taught were from their college-level offerings, and they required depth of thought beyond what I was used to as a high school student. I had never formally studied philosophy or foreign relations, and I struggled with the philosophical mode of reasoning so new to me. The two classes were especially enjoyable because of the amount of student input allowed by the professors. Often classes became absorbing debates on issues between opposing factions of students. The foreign policy professor gave me a less biased understanding of world affairs and hardened my resolve to explore his field in college.

Governor's School mirrored university life because we were given virtual freedom outside of the classroom. "Homework" assignments were free of accountability, and not all extracurricular seminars and speeches were mandatory. Creating and being solely responsible for one's own schedule are perhaps the most important skills required in higher education, and Governor's School was an ideal environment in which to learn that discipline.

One of Governor's School's greatest challenges was to join a diverse group of strangers and try to come to know as many of them as possible. I have attended only one school all of my life, and developing new friends, many with backgrounds different from mine, will be an important goal for me at the beginning of college. Governor's School was good preparation for the flood of faces and personalities that I will be caught up in on a large campus.

I believe that I have had unusual opportunities for emotional and intellectual growth on top of the strong, caring, and constant support North Cross has given to me for thirteen years. I hope Duke might be the next important step in my development and a lifelong loyalty.

—CARR MCCLAIN

COMMENT: Carr manages to discuss two very different events—his reaction to his sister's death and his experience at Virginia's Governor's School—in a single, unified essay. His thesis sentence includes both events in a rational manner: he tells the readers he will discuss two major causes of intellectual and emotional growth.

*   *   *

I will never forget the sound of skull hitting pavement, or the sight of the bleeding, unconscious man lying in the middle of the street. Was he dead? He certainly wasn't moving, and he seemed to be bleeding an awful lot from the huge gash in his head. During a slow selling hour at my flower cart in downtown Boston, I happened to be watching the traffic on the nearby main street when I saw a man punch another man hard in the jaw. The man who was hit fell straight and hard onto the concrete, and now lay unconscious amid the traffic.

But the offender didn't stay to see any of this. Instead, he simply turned, abandoning the scene that he had created. How did he know that he hadn't killed that man? The immobile body lying on the pavement gave no outward signs of consciousness. How did he know, that in his moment of rage, he hadn't committed a murder?

Even when it was over, I didn't stop thinking about it. I was still thinking about it for days afterward. I think about it now. It was the first act of violence I had ever seen take place right in front of me. At first, I couldn't understand it. How could a man punch another man in the middle of the street for no obvious reason? And how could he just walk away? Physical violence, to me, is a last resort—a way to defend myself if someone attacks me. I don't think I would ever initiate the violence; my conscience wouldn't let me. Now, months after the incident, I do see, at least, that to some people initiating the violence is acceptable. For example, the man obviously felt that he had reason enough to hit the other man, that he was justified—so he did. This perspective, although still difficult, is easier to condone in my mind than his walking away—the part I simply couldn't understand. How one man could injure another man so badly that he was no longer conscious is so totally opposed to my own sense of values that at the time I couldn't comprehend it. It is completely alien to what I believe to be right, to my idea of morality.

It was surprising, but most of all frightening to see the discrepancy between my views and his. I suddenly realized that I have been living only at my end of the moral spectrum all this time, unconsciously using it as a kind of shelter protecting me from reality. This reality is not easy to accept—the sudden awareness that my sense of right and wrong, my morality, has been shaped by a contained, controlled environment, and that this environment, although secure, has hidden from me the attitude—the lack of concern for the life of another person— that scared me most in this incident. This realization is the part I still think about. And this is the part I am only beginning to understand.

I guess I am starting to recognize that I am losing the neat, uncomplicated view of things I once had. I am beginning to see that as time goes by I will be exposed to more incidents that will make this realization even clearer. But I may never stop thinking about the man at the flower cart, and I may never fully understand.

—LYDIA MAGLIOZZI

COMMENT: The skull hitting the pavement in the first line will catch the reader's attention. The precisely observed and recorded development of the writer's own thinking will probably impress the committee.

* * *

Anticipation filled with excitement, anxiety, and doubt all took turns with my still digesting breakfast keeping me on the edge of my desk waiting for the moment of my exaltation or misery. Acceptance into the junior Honors English class would have been an honor and a sort of reward for all the hard work and effort I had placed in my sophomore English class. The challenge of working with classmates and teachers who would constantly test my abilities to speak, write, and interpret literature enticed my interests and hopes.

At a slow, agonizing pace Mr. Abel, my sophomore English teacher, walked down each aisle and in careful detail explained to each student his grade and for some whether or not they were accepted into the honors course. As soon as Mr. Abel came to my desk I knew my knotted stomach was not without cause, because his usual jovial gestures and speech were replaced by a solemn and reserved tone. "Matt," Mr. Abel deliberately said, "after careful consideration I have decided not to recommend you for the honors course because I feel you would not be happy." Having someone drop an anvil on your forehead would probably best describe the speechless and confused state in which I finished the rest of my morning classes. My brown bag lunch and large Coke failed to settle my disturbed nerves because I continually asked myself over and over why would I not be happy, what led him to believe this, and what weaknesses in my abilities does he see? During lunch my best friend was overflowing with pride and self-importance because he too had encountered Mr. Abel and deservedly was accepted into the honors class because he had earned an A+ in Mr. Abel's class and was by far one of the better writers in the class. His sympathy for my predicament only seemed to fuel my burning anger, but it also added to my confusion because I became unsure whether I was angry at myself, Mr. Abel, or my classmates who had been accepted.

After aimlessly wandering the halls outside the English Office attempting to evaluate why I was not accepted and hoping to throw together a presentable argument that might change Mr. Abel's mind, I timidly slipped into the English Office and cautiously confronted Mr. Abel. "Mr. Abel," I said slowly gaining confidence as I spoke, "I do not understand your decision. I earned A's in your class and I believe my writing and class participation is up to or better than some who have been accepted. I do not . . ." "Matt, you have to understand," interrupted Mr. Abel, "that I have not chosen all of the students, their own teachers have, and it is my professional opinion that you would be happier in a regular junior English course because you would be more comfortable standing out in that course instead of being just another student in the honors class."

Having someone who I admire and respect as a person who also is my English teacher hand me the first academic rejection of my life just stymied me. Because I trusted his opinion, I could not allow myself to be vengeful towards Mr. Abel, but I would not allow his opinion the remotest chance of breaking my confidence in my ability.

Although I forced myself through a series of painful self-evaluations trying to determine whether or not Mr. Abel was right, I would not admit to myself that he could be right. That night before I went to sleep, I promised myself that by completely committing all of my efforts and abilities to success in my junior English class I would show Mr. Abel I was qualified for the senior Honors English course.

Such a singular goal in my English class could have strangled any educational gains in my junior year, instead I broadened my involvement in application of my skills by writing various articles for the school newspaper ranging from athletics to featured articles on the front page, joining the writing staff on the yearbook, and composing poetry for the literary magazine. In addition to finding enjoyment in writing for the newspaper, yearbook and literary magazine, I was transformed in my approach to English class from working hard for a grade to finding pleasure both in my writing and in interpreting literature.

Now I find myself in the senior Honors English class that I had promised myself; however, my selfish goal of proving to Mr. Abel that his decision was wrong has changed. Our student-teacher relationship, I feel, has grown into a strong bond and any initial bitter feelings have long since been replaced by a true sense of friendship. Through this experience I have learned a simple but effective form of self-evaluation which has helped me keep a clear and focused view of my motivations and goals, and I feel I have learned how to handle adversity maturely and objectively.

—MATTHEW DEGREEFF

COMMENT: Many applicants write about turning a defeat into a victory. Few take the risk that Matthew did: he records an academic defeat in his application to a very academic school. His essay succeeds in part because he eventually succeeded. But the essay's success derives to a greater extent from the judicious tone Matt uses and his ability to look at himself and his situation with some objectivity.

*   *   *

I knew it was okay to cry. I had listened attentively when the judges told me, with sympathy in their eyes, that it was normal to be distressed. But I wasn't going to subject myself to misery solely because of contemporary societal expectations. Kids are supposed to be happy—unconditionally happy—and that was the only expectation that I was going to fulfill. My parents' divorce wasn't going to crush me. It wasn't going to grieve me. It wasn't even going to penetrate my protective outer shell. I had built that outer shell just too strong. I was an eleven year old "Stone Boy" climbing out, untouched, from the wreckage of an apparently destroyed family. I was my family's only survivor. Everyone else had given in to the maudlin emotions which could only lead to their unhappiness. If I didn't feel anything, I certainly wasn't going to feel pain. So I decided not to feel anything.

My family had failed; I hadn't and I knew that. It wasn't fair that I should suffer because of a colossal mistake that my parents had made. My family ship was sinking and all aboard were going to suffer dearly. To survive, you latched firmly on to the hand of the captain who you vowed your loyalty to and looked on pitifully, sorrowfully to the other captain, wondering what was going to happen to her and her beloved crew. That was the expected choice: to pick custody of one and ostensibly betray the other. Well, that was too big of a choice for me at eleven because I loved both captains. So I chose not to choose; chose not to feel; chose not to care. If I wasn't part of the family, I couldn't be affected by its disasters. So I chose not to be part of the family. And I died.

For eight months, I watched as my family mourned the death of itself and I wondered why they would subject themselves to such painful feelings. I became stoical and relished in the calmness of my indifference. I became a rock; an island. Eight months later, however, the bulk of the storm had passed and my family was recovering from its breakup. During this period, I had become completely unemotional and had detached myself from my family. I could not love these people anymore. I had separated myself from them to ensure my own survival, but they, by not separating from each other, had survived. When I realized how totally alone I had become, I began to cry for myself and didn't stop until I had cried for my family and their misery that I had not been a part of. Here, I began to feel again. Here, I became capable of loving my family again. Finally, here is where I accepted my parents' divorce.

I've read that psychologists conclude that there are five stages in the acceptance of any death: denial, anger, bargaining, depression, and acceptance. There is no given length which a person must remain in each stage but each invariably must be passed through. In the death of my family, I remained in the denial stage for eight lonely months and passed through the next four stages in two hours. I didn't realize that in order to feel pleasure, one must feel pain. And if you cut off all feeling, you lose both of them.

—MATT KOSTER

COMMENT: An arresting opening, a sensitive exploration of a painful experience, combined with objectivity aided by outside information.

WRITING ABOUT POLITICAL AND SOCIAL INVOLVEMENT

Essays which express the applicant's social or political involvement are often extremely effective and powerful. Michael Millender of Duke discusses a local Atlanta issue, building the Carter Library and Park. He tells of the community opposition and his own reaction to the project. Harvard College's Lisa Schkolnick writes of her ideals and involvements in Amnesty International and Church World Service CROP. Next, two students write about the nuclear freeze movement. First a Wisconsin student argues against a nuclear freeze, then Vilashini Coppan of Yale University discusses the organizing of a STOP seminar at Wellesley High School. Craig Steffee who attended the North Carolina School of Science and Math and is now at Duke University, discusses health care policy, its responsibility to society and the individual. Finally, Etan Diamond of Block Yeshiva High School and the University of Pennsylvania defines the word "success" in terms of personal goals and Talmudic teachings.

*   *   *

For the past several years, the proposed construction of Jimmy Carter's Presidential Library and its accompanying four-lane highway in the middle of Atlanta's historic residential area has wrapped the city in debate and controversy. As the issue grew, I found myself drawn to it not only because the road will be located near my school, but also because of my interest in Atlanta's past; my historical perspective and desire to save my city's heritage have made me strongly opposed to the project.

The road and library would be built in the Great Park, a wasteland of condemned property overgrown with kudzu where houses were demolished several years ago in preparation for another, since-abandoned highway project. Beginning down-town, the road would cut through the Great Park, go past the Presidential Library, and then empty its traffic one hundred feet from my school. Proponents of the road claim that it would provide access to the library as well as a quick route downtown, something Atlanta sorely needs. However, community opposition to the project has been vehement and well-organized. Protest groups have been formed, a legal battle is being waged, and one cannot drive through the area without seeing bumper stickers bearing slogans such as "Save, Don't Pave!" and my favorite, "Take It to Plains, Jimmy!" Even little children, in a reference to the head of the Georgia Department of Transportation, chant "Tom Moreland is a toad—We don't want his stupid road!"

My first reaction to the proposed highway was concern over its proximity to my school. One plan calls for the road to end at an intersection next to my school; another would have the highway lanes angle off and merge into the existing street. Either alternative would create excessive traffic that would be dangerous for young children walking home or to the bus stop. Needless to say, the noise from the highway would not be welcomed by anyone attempting to study or take a test.

I found further reasons to oppose the highway once I examined its impact on the surrounding historic neighborhoods. Blessed with an abundance of land and cheap labor, Atlanta's Victorian residents were never confined to apartments or rowhouses. They built large neighborhoods with impressive main thoroughfares, plentiful and easily accessible parks, and tree-lined sidestreets. One such neighborhood was designed by Frederick Law Olmsted, the famous landscape architect. Even today his parkway is intact, though the mansions along it are now home to such diverse groups as schools, a yoga center, and a Mormon church. The caution exercised by the area's residents has allowed their community to adapt to the modern world while retaining its historic character and design. Despite this prudent flexibility that best exemplifies preservation in

Atlanta, the area would be irreparably damaged by the road's construction. Hundred-year-old streets would be torn up and rerouted, parks would be destroyed, and the road itself would be a scar cutting through the entire community. I understand the concerns expressed by Atlanta officials as they face the prospect of a growing city with overburdened and inadequate highways, but I feel there are ways the Great Park could be developed that would meet their interests without damaging the surrounding community. A rail line similar to ones in other parts of the city could efficiently move people downtown with minimal environmental impact. The Great Park could then be turned into a *real* park with the Presidential Library at its center. Atlanta's historic neighborhoods have shown that they can change as the city around them changes, but this does not give us a license to rashly destroy them for the sake of progress. I hope that the city's builders and preservationists can together find a means of saving yesterday and at the same time provide for tomorrow.

—Michael Millender

*   *   *

It was late afternoon as I sat on the edge of the reflecting pool and dipped my feet in the tepid water. Absent-mindedly I wiped my forehead with the back of my arm. It had been a long August day, vintage Washington D.C., swelteringly hot and muggy. I had been carrying homemade signs denouncing nuclear proliferation and human rights abuses. As this was the twentieth anniversary of Martin Luther King Jr.'s 1963 March on Washington, I was proudly sporting a pin that urged, "Don't let the dream die."

I began to fear, however, that there was a dream dying inside me. I had expected to experience a sort of catharsis at this march. I had wanted to be free of the individualism and cynicism of the present decade, but I could not escape it. I longed to feel the unity that people told me had existed in 1963, but instead I felt rather empty and alone.

What, after all, was I accomplishing by joining a quarter-of-a-million people standing in the hot sun shouting protests to the world? President Reagan was not even in town; he seemed oblivious to our concerns and supplications. And what would happen after this day? I would return to Princeton, where I had been born and lived all my life. In a couple of weeks I would return to school, joining hundreds of my peers, many of whom might not have heard or cared about the march. What would my ideals mean then?

Despite my disappointment I realized that at least the personal ideals that had brought me to Washington were still within me. Besides, I reasoned, charity begins at home. I recalled the time, in my sophomore year, when someone with whom I had been friends in junior high was hospitalized with an eating disorder. I was shocked and saddened, and I felt incredibly sorry that it had been a long time since I had spoken to this girl.

I wrote a letter, and when my old friend wrote back I wrote again and again, eager to help her through this difficult time. Once I even visited her in the hospital in New York. I was a little frightened by her emaciated arms and her pallor, but I felt happy afterwards. It was good to talk to her, and even though when she came home we drifted apart again, I felt fulfilled in that I done what I could for her when it was important.

Just as I care deeply for those who are or who have been close to me, I continue to care for those whom I have never met, but who need me nonetheless. The far-away cries of the hungry and of political prisoners have affected me most.

I thought about my two years of coordinating groups of high school students in an effort to raise money to help the world's hungry through Church World Service CROP. Together each October we have walked ten miles. We have wondered about the lives and dreams of people starving in Niger and Bolivia, and we have wondered if those who are malnourished in Trenton know how much we care.

But when I get home from a peace march or a CROP walk there are still people undergoing electric shocks, being beaten, or being verbally abused hour upon hour. To assist these victims I send letters around the world. Politely and firmly I address myself to presidents and prime ministers, urging them to adhere to the United Nations Universal Declaration of Human Rights and even, in some cases, their own nations' constitutions. I find my correspondence with and my increased understanding of other nations both intellectually stimulating and emotionally satisfying.

If there is one thing I have learned from my active involvement in Amnesty International it is that no matter how much I do for others, no matter how much I give of myself, it will never be enough to compensate for the failures of men and women to help each other and themselves. All I can do is make some small contribution to that idealistic goal of "saving the world." I struggle with the side of me that argues that causes are either corrupt or hopeless. It is up to me to make them honest and promising—a task I accept joyously and without regret. How could I allow all the love I feel to go to waste?

My misgivings about the true efficacy of my efforts on behalf of my society and my world ultimately have served to strengthen my resolve. However often I must, in the future, stand in a hot summer sun, tired and perspiring, I will be soothed and gladdened by thoughts of the people I am helping. If those people can be even a little better off for what I have done, my personal dream will never die.

—LISA SCHKOLNICK

COMMENT: "How much difference does an individual make?" Lisa asks. She answers that an individual can make a difference, but the thrust of her essay is personal, not abstract. Her determination to continue her involvement in causes, even if the benefits are slight, suggests her ability to apply theory to her own life. Specific references to specific causes help here.

* * *

The United States is presently embroiled in a debate concerning nuclear disarmament and our nation's defense policy. Thousands of well-intentioned citizens in this country and Europe have joined left-wing radicals to denounce the strengthening of America's nuclear deterrent. They have been joined by politicians who have boarded the nuclear freeze bandwagon either out of sincere, albeit misguided principle, or, quite possibly, for political self-aggrandizement. Most of the freeze supporters are interested in peace, which is admirable, but their vehicle for peace, the freeze, would only increase the possibility of nuclear war.

One of the main problems with the freeze is that it would do exactly what it says; freeze U.S. and Soviet forces at their present, unbalanced level. The freeze would leave the Soviets almost twice the nuclear megatonnage of the U.S., and the very frightening capability to destroy the U.S. land based missiles, a capability we do not presently possess. If deranged Soviet leadership were ever to use this capability, the only option for a U.S. president would be a strike at Soviet population centers with America's weaker submarine and air-launched missiles. This response would in turn lead to an attack on the U.S. population centers by the Soviets. Whether an American president would strike back under these circumstances is suspect. This all too real scenario is the major reason we need an invulnerable MX system, an impossibility with the freeze.

Another major flaw with the freeze is the point of verification. The Russians have consistently violated previous treaties, especially concerning chemical toxins, and there is no reason to believe that they would exercise good faith with this treaty either. Another major drawback to the nuclear freeze is that with a freeze in place, the Russians would have no incentive to negotiate for a reduction in nuclear arms. With their advantage frozen in place, the Russians would feel secure that any American weapons systems, such as the MX or cruise missile, which could reinstate parity, would be impossible. They would have no desire to reduce their own superiority. A freeze would also allow the Soviets to retain their total nuclear domination in Europe.

What America needs is not a freeze at present unsafe levels, but instead a continued drive toward parity in conjunction with serious negotiations concerning arms reductions. A freeze would be a palliative to the American people, curing their emotional fear of nuclear war, but allowing the possibility of such a war to fester and grow.

—ANONYMOUS

COMMENT: Well-argued and intelligent, but revealing little of the writer. This was one of several for an application; the others perhaps revealed the writer.

*   *   *

Two months ago, I co-organized a four day seminar upon the issues of nuclear weapons and nuclear war, working within my capacity as secretary and press contact for Wellesley High School's Student Teacher Organization for the Prevention of Nuclear War (STOP). When planning the schedule of events, I felt it vital that STOP appear merely as an organization of concerned individuals, devoid of iron labels and political connotations. In accordance with this ideal, I scheduled speakers and performers from a variety of political and occupational backgrounds, in addition to inviting speakers who support views contrary to those of the anti-nuclear movement. When developing the symposium, I attempted to present a general overview of the issue of nuclear war while simultaneously examining certain points of interest, such as the statistical effects of a hypothetical nuclear attack, and the current state of the American-Soviet arms race. I perceived the seminar not as an endeavor to convert students to STOP's particular opinions and ideals, but rather as an opportunity to rationally persuade students to begin to confront the existing threat of nuclear war. Ideally, STOP should attempt to appeal to students' sense of logic rather than bombarding the students with a barrage of fear and terror regarding the consequences of a nuclear war. Involvement and action must be a personal choice, the result of the logical consideration of both sides of an issue.

Were STOP to present only one side of the controversy surrounding nuclear weapons, it seems that the organization would negate its very attempt to raise awareness on this issue. Awareness implies both knowledge and choice; an exposure to the entirety of a question. Therefore, I arranged for a Soviet dissident and the Director of the Massachusetts Civil Defense Agency, both of whom favor peace through strength, to address the school. In addition, I scheduled debates upon the issues of a proposed nuclear weapons freeze, and the Soviet perspective on arms control and usage.

In order to further expand Wellesley's STOP character, I intend to participate in an internship with the adult Boston area offices of STOP and Educators for Social Responsibility next semester. Presently, Wellesley High School's STOP chapter is somewhat of a non-entity amongst other school organizations; during the past year STOP has consisted of six active members in a student body of approximately twelve hundred. Apathy is the precursor of destruction; therefore, I see it as essential that students and adults start to acknowledge and confront the possibility of a nuclear catastrophe.

My involvement with STOP has enabled me to better apprehend the necessity for comprehension rather than blind condemnation of a particular viewpoint. By speaking with representatives of both sides of the nuclear weapons issues, I have realized that those who advocate peace through military strength cannot be defined as simply "war-crazed" any more than the anti-nuclear movement can be defined as "liberal." Judging from conversations I have had with students, STOP is often seen as a group of incensed liberals and/or radicals. The majority of students tend to dismiss or avoid the organization, thus failing to perceive the central issue itself. Obviously, the threat of nuclear war and subsequent global destruction transcends such political stratifications, as it also transcends all other barriers. It is this universal appeal for the survival of the planet that I wish to convey to students and adults in my work with STOP.

—VILASHINI COPPAN

COMMENT: The topic is global, but Vilashini has made the topic manageable by focussing on a specific issue—making STOP apolitical—and by focussing on her involvement and responsibilities. She's narrowed the topic, and she's emphasized her personal involvement in the issues. She could have helped the reader by providing rests from the long sentences.

*   *   *

Nearly every policy issue in the field of health care can be condensed into financial and/or ethical arguments pitting the rights of the individual against the interests of society at large. The question of who should prevail in policy considerations thus becomes the issue central to the entire field of health care policy.

The government, as the primary health care policy-making body, must interpret its responsibility to "the people" as it applies to the individual patient and to society as a whole. It must function as a protective organization; the right of each person to health care must not be denied through lack of funds, yet the economic well-being of society should not be disrupted to expand without bound the technological limits of medical science.

The "free market" system of health care, whereby the patient pays the physician (health care provider) directly for his services, produces a unique financial contract and bond of trust between the health care system and the individual. Thus, the physician's duty is strongly oriented to the wishes of the individual patient, despite the cost to society of focusing extraordinary care on one person. The cost of medical care is effectively shared by the entire population through insurance companies and direct state aid administered by the government.

The government and all creators of health care policy however, must examine not only the patient's right to the highest "quality of life" achievable but also must scrutinize the resulting costs to society. Health care policymakers must assume the dual role of protecting the economic structure of society and providing financial access to proper health care for every individual in the population. On a given issue, they must obligate their priorities to either the individual patient or society. The choice of either as the prime concern in a health care policy, however, inflicts a toll on the other party.

Society's interest in medical practices centers around the rationing of health care dollars/technology and the sanctity of prolonged life; with such a schizoid attitude, policy issues can be interpreted as purely economic questions (the greatest benefit to the greatest number of productive individuals) or as an unrealistic desire to maximize lifespan (will more people survive their illness) if the autonomy of individual patients is not honored. Economic concerns may be pursued most effectively through the loss of personal freedoms, but this is impossible due to obvious ethical contradictions—i.e., euthanasia or denial of care for nonproductive individuals.

Concentration on the interests of the individual leads to the loss of national economic potential through the cost of advanced care administered to individuals who will never rejoin the work force. The judiciary branch of the government must thus intercede as a protective element against the needless prolongation of terminal or degenerative illness. Within the framework of the courts, the legal basis of medicine has been interpreted as responsibility to the individual's decision of acceptance or denial of care. This has been brought to light by cases of minors, mental incompetents, and patients not able to make their own decisions. In such cases, the physician has been instructed to sacrifice society's ethical concept of prolonging life at any cost in favor of the desires of the individual.

As in any technological system, socioeconomic and regional variations in the level of care available mandate that difficult choices be made to improve health care or to incorporate new technology—such choices must be made on the basis of financial repercussions as well as personal/professional ethics.

Neither the individual physician nor a group of health care professionals alone can devise health care policy without external review; this would legislate the values, ethics, and self-interests of a particular profession. Society as a whole, however, remains undereducated regarding the science and procedures of health care; the general public is thus in a dubious position to unilaterally dictate health care policy. Public health policies must thus be formulated by a mixed group of professionals and non-professionals balancing the interests of society and the rights of the individual within the constraints of medical ethics and standard health care procedures.

—CRAIG STEFFEE

*   *   *

The word "success" immediately evokes an image of education, power and wealth. Whether it be the school one attended, the type of vice-presidency one has attained in a company, or the number of cars a person has, any of these status symbols are a sure sign of success. The Talmud, the

Jewish Code of Law, agrees that these three characteristics are part of the success combination. But it gives different measurements of education, power and wealth: "Who is wise? He who learns from his fellow man. Who is powerful? He who overcomes his desires. Who is rich? He who is happy with his share." By developing, in this order, each of these pieces of advice, a person can very easily become successful in all that he does.

"Who is wise? He who learns from his fellow man." Although education is very important, an education without a certain amount of wisdom is worthless. What this saying means is that there is always something new to learn from every person, be it some sort of ethical lesson or a practical piece of advice. Therefore, no one should think of himself as so intelligent and smart that he cannot be advised by someone "lower." This is especially helpful in the business world, where people are advised constantly. If a person can accept this advice and develop a sense of learning from his fellow man, he can work more successfully. After developing this wisdom, a person can also move to the next step for success.

"Who is powerful? He who overcomes his desires." After a person acquires this wisdom and begins to settle into his job, visions of advancement on the job ladder are always imminent. Becoming president or chief executive officer is the dream. But unfortunately, some people do not have the maturity to pace themselves in achieving this dream. Unethical business practices and sometimes even illegal dealings can become part of their work, as they try to get ahead of the competition. The appropriate way is to develop a frame of business morals in which one should operate. Desires to get ahead should not completely overwhelm a person to the point of undermining principles. With this developed sense of ethics and wisdom, a person can now successfully fulfill the third step to success.

"Who is rich? He who is happy with his lot." Most of the business world and life in general revolves around money. Some people have a lot, and some people do not. But whatever the amount of money one has, it should not be the single most important factors in a person's life. Its importance should not, for example, encourage people to commit criminal actions to get more. Also, money should not drive people crazy when they cannot get enough of it. If someone has developed the wisdom to learn from others, he will see that other people can live comfortably on lesser amounts of money. If he has developed his power to overcome his desires, he will understand that what he has is enough.

These three steps, although not the common ways to achieve success, are probably the right ways for me. Hopefully, as I mature, I will develop the discipline to reach each of these steps. I would also like to add a fourth step . . . the need for a balanced lifestyle. I would like to take time to enjoy my family, friends, and new experiences. This fourth step will balance and reinforce the first three steps. Whatever career I eventually choose, these steps should help me deal with other people and with myself.

—ETAN DIAMOND

COMMENT: Reading to the end of this essay pays off. In the last paragraph, Etan connects the rather abstract discussion to his own life, and the reader can see that the discourse has personal meaning. But what if the reader gave up reading before the end?

WRITING ABOUT FAMILY MEMBERS AND FRIENDS

The source of inspiration of a good essay is often close at hand. The following essays explore relationships with family members and friends. Neal and Mark Fishbach, whose essays reflect upon the meaning of being a twin, are both attending the University of Pennsylvania. While their essays are based on the same subject, they are remarkably different in content and focus. Haverford College's Amelia Kohm writes of her mother's strong emotional support. Next, an anonymous Yale student discusses the great value that she has placed upon friendships, stressing the qualities that she considers important in any relationship. Jill Troy of Stanford University tells of a classmate's dedication to working on their school's newspaper, emphasizing the positive influence that that student has had on Jill's life. Finally, Randi S. Chervitz's essay attempts to analyze her generation's apparent sense of conservatism. Randi is now at Vassar College.

*　*　*

Statistics show that three out of every one thousand pregnancies result in identical twins. I was lucky enough to be one of the three, and after seventeen years I still feel lucky. Some psychologists believe that growing up as an identical twin hinders the maturing process. My own opinion is that besides being exceptional fun, being an identical twin has been the most positive and enriching element of my growing up.

One reason my experience as a twin has been so positive is that my brother, Mark, and I compete in a constructive, encouraging way, while avoiding the bitter sibling rivalry that plagues so many others. Competition does not exist in the winner and loser sense. Rather than burn each other's home-

175

work, or cut holes in each other's baseball mitts, we push each other to higher achievements. If Mark sprints the last 2 laps of a grueling swim practice, instead of taking it easy, I sprint out after him. The next day he might be the tired one and I might be the one to encourage that last beneficial lap. Likewise in school, if Mark studies that extra hour late at night, I make an effort to sit down and concentrate. The unique aspect of this mutual motivation is that we never attempt anything simply to be "better" than the other. I have absolutely no desire to know who's the better athlete, who's smarter, or who's stronger. Rather than compete against each other, I think we compete for each other. I like to think the only competition between us serves to bring out our best efforts, not to determine who has the upper hand.

Socially, being a twin has provided a lot of laughs, and a lot of support. Aside from small benefits, such as switching classes or dates, having a reliable, constant companion has made my progress through childhood incalculably easier. When our family moved from Boston to St. Louis as I began my eighth grade in 1981, being a twin protected me from some of the intense fears a single child might experience. Of course the move was not easy. As I remember, I was not overly enthusiastic about leaving, but I never experienced the fear of being alone in a strange place. I had my brother as a companion for those first few days of settling in. Today I like to think I am adaptable enough to handle any situation, but in the eighth grade having a twin was tremendously helpful.

More importantly than the social benefits, having a twin brother has encouraged me to develop my own individuality and sense of identity. Whether it be a conscious effort to dress differently, or to select different courses, we have made a definite effort to appear as two individuals. This "quest" for individuality has at times been difficult. When I was younger I felt a definite comfort and security in being alike, but in the past few years I have felt a stronger need to be unique. Today when I look at my brother, I see past the striking, but obvious similarities, and I am aware that important internal differences exist. I have become comfortable with my distinct identity, a debt I owe partially to my brother. To sum it up in one sentence, I would not trade my twin experience. A small Carribbean island with 50 wives might be tempting, but in the end not as satisfying. With the imminence of college and the end of my legal childhood, some difficult decisions must be made that will undoubtedly effect my relationship with my brother. Will we go to the same college? Will we go to colleges in the same state? Will we even go to colleges on the same coast? Yet confronted with an uncertain future, there is one thing of which I can always be sure. I will always have a reliable, understanding, encouraging twin brother. No distance or amount of time can change that fact, and with this security I will certainly be happy with whatever the future brings.

—NEAL FISHBACH

* * *

What's it like being a twin? Oedipus would have needed more than a ribbon to solve this conundrum. After being a twin for 17 years, however, I feel I'm qualified to provide an answer.

Being a twin is just plain fun. Not just because I can pick my brother's date up at the door, but because I enjoy being with him. We like the same music, food, sports and types of people. Sure my brother Neal may like blondes while I prefer brunettes, but we're still extremely compatible. Because we're alike in many respects, I find that friends made by one of us quickly take to the other. Thus as a twin, our circle of friends is geometrically increased.

Mutual generosity and sharing is a large part of our twinship. If two unequal portions of pie were left on the table, neither one of us would grab for the bigger slice. In fact, there would be dive for the less attractive piece. This desire to see the other happy and, ultimately, successful leads to teamwork. When making difficult decisions, rather than write "Dear Abby," I can turn to Neal. Likewise Neal has his own resident Ann Landers.

In areas where ability levels differ, the stronger one of us, out of desire to see the other succeed, works to make the weaker better than himself. The weaker, by the same token, works just as hard to insure that the other continues to improve. What results is a constantly upward trend in our abilities. Academically, the presence of a "peer tutor" within shouting range not only has saved much time and energy, it has also enhanced our comprehension of material.

While having a twin is fantastic, fun and helpful, I do not need to be with him in order to succeed. My experience at the Andover Summer School verified this. Although my brother also attended Andover, he did not take the same courses as I did, did not live remotely close to where I lived, and did not have the same free time that I had. Still, my Andover summer was one of the best I've had. By becoming more open, and exerting that extra effort, I made many lasting friends, in addition to learning a great deal. In a sense, my trip to summer school was as much a test of my social independence as it was of my academic ability.

Few things distress me more than being called half a person. I have always worked to establish my own identity—my own likes and dislikes. Just because many of these coincide with my brother's does not mean we are the same person. Neither do I wish to be exactly like Neal. Sure, I sometimes wish I was also right handed so I could play second base, but I'm happy to play first or the outfield.

Being a twin has been the most enriching experience of my life. Never will I be alone. Yet always will I ask the question, what is it like *not* being a twin?

—MARK FISHBACH

* * *

"Give them hell, Amy!" I've heard my mother say this to me all through my life. I can hear her telling me this as I walked out the door to face the peer pressures of fifth and sixth grade, my first exams at high school, my first day of a real job, or just any normal school day. Now, when I think of my mother telling an eleven year old to "give them hell," I laugh, but this cheer of confidence is typical of how my mother has treated me, and I feel she has had a great influence on my life.

Perhaps what makes my mother's unconditional love and confidence even more special is that she didn't receive the same kind of support during her childhood. My grandparents, who are vivacious and loving people, never gained a great degree of confidence in themselves. Both my grandmother and grandfather grew up in poor families. Although through hard work they became successful, I don't think they ever became confident enough in their success to stop feeling the need to prove themselves. Because of their lack of confidence, they were unable to give my mother a great deal of support. My mother, who now works as a counselor for parents, has recognized her parents' weakness, gained self-confidence through her work, and has not passed on the legacy of insecurity to her children.

My mother's undying confidence in me has helped me through some of the hardest adjustments in my life. No matter how many bad things happened to me, I never felt like a bad person. In grade school some of my friends and I underwent a good deal of social exclusion. I struggled through the first great challenge to my self esteem without much grace, and at times I felt undesirable and dull. However, I never felt that all this was happening to me because I deserved it. Although I might have been temporarily dented, I was not permanently damaged. In addition to helping me through rough times, the confidence my mother instilled in me has helped me take risks and leave home. I find it easier to take risks knowing that I have a strong foundation built at home.

Above all, I am beginning to learn how to give support to others as my mother has given it to me. Through my work with children at a day care center and at a summer camp in Michigan, I see that children are more willing to take risks and learn if they are given plenty of cheers of confidence. They gain a positive, confident feeling about themselves that helps them pull through the rough spots. Moreover, my mother and I have become friends who cheer each other on. As my mother is leaving to give a lecture or to go on a business trip, I say, "Give them hell, Mom."

—AMELIA KOHM

*   *   *

I have always placed a great value and importance on my friendships, and an experience which has deeply affected and influenced my life, and which has taught me a great deal about people, has been my relationship with a dear friend. In order to understand why friends hold such meaning for me, however, I feel it is first necessary to describe, if only briefly, the circumstances of my upbringing.

When I was growing up, my older brother, who was extremely shy and introverted, took up a great deal of my parents' time and worry. I saw two things as a child which deeply impressed me: my brother's dependence on my parents, and his apparent lack of friends. My brother's childhood experiences affected me so deeply that I must have determined at a very early age to be relatively independent of my family so that my parents would not have to worry about me in the way that they did of my brother. Another priority which I established fairly early in life was the importance of having good friends. I felt strongly about the necessity of close friends, partly because my brother had so few and partly because, as I tended to conceal my problems or preoccupations from my parents, I needed people that I could confide in who would give me support when I needed it. Consequently, the word "friend" carries a great significance for me. I feel that a friendship requires sincere concern for each other's well-being and, at times, involves sacrifice (just as any important relationship does). My friends have always been relatively few in number, but very close. Two specific relationships with friends have been particularly influential in my life, although they were completely opposite in nature.

As a freshman in high school, I became friends with a girl named Rita. Rita seemed to live life for the sole purpose of enjoying it. She was full of witty humor and sparkling enthusiasm; I had always been very serious-minded and introspective. She was the sort of person that was easy to have fun with, for any occasion was always filled with her laughter and amusing remarks. Yet, as the year progressed, I slowly gained insights into Rita which were very painful. She was incapable of having a serious intellectual or emotional conversation. Although I perceived that she felt strongly about certain things, she always attempted to hide all of her emotions. She never discussed her problems or concerns with me, nor did she wish me to share mine with her. This total lack of communication was extremely frustrating for me since I already considered Rita a very good friend. Although I realize now that Rita simply had a completely different outlook on life from my own and a different concept of what friends should be, at the time I felt extremely saddened and disillusioned. I was totally confused by people who were incapable of expressing emotions and who dismissed friendships so lightly.

It was not until my junior year that I was able to gain any insight into this experience. When I joined our high school yearbook, I had the opportunity to meet many new people whom I would never otherwise have known. Among these people was the Editor-in-Chief of the yearbook. Meg and I soon realized that we shared many of the same interests, values, and concerns. We rapidly became good friends, and it is this relationship which has most deeply affected my life. Meg, unlike Rita, was willing to have serious conversations and to discuss subjects of very personal significance. She placed great importance on all the relationships in her life, from family to friends. She cared sincerely about her editors on the yearbook, even those who were not her personal friends. She often sacrificed her time to help others, whether an editor who needed help with his section or a friend who needed advice. Most important to me, she offered constant encouragement and support, and helped me to understand people, such as Jennifer, who were different from me.

I have learned many things from my friendship with Meg. I learned, from her tolerance and patience with others, that people are truly different and unique individuals, and that the differences between some people are virtually absolute and include opposing values, views, and philosophies. Yet there is no correct view on life, and one person can not in any way blame another for being different from himself; nor can he demand of another more than that person is willing or able to give. I am once again friends with Rita, and enjoy her company when several of our circle of friends go out together. I do not ask her to share with me her fears or anxieties, nor do I speak of my own with her. I no longer try to force her to be something that she is not, but recognize that she has her own personality, vastly different from mine.

However, I have also realized from my friendship with Meg how important my own values are to me. I hope that I may grow to be the type of person that Meg is, because she exemplifies the qualities which I have always held important. I, like Meg, consider it essential to care about other people, to be able to share dreams, fears, and ambitions, and to be willing to make sacrifices for others when necessary. I realize that this view of friends is very idealistic, but I feel that people must always work to achieve the ideal; as long as we continue to struggle for the best in life, we can be confident that we are making progress.

—ANONYMOUS

COMMENT: This writer realizes that one can often define oneself by defining others. By looking at her friends, she looks at herself. But some concrete, specific experiences (e.g., Rita lends "constant encouragement and support"—how?) would help the reader, who does not know the people depicted.

* * *

Susie turned in her seat and leaned toward the radiator to secretly read the latest issue of our school newspaper, *Tom-Tom*. She wore her *Tom-Tom* shirt proudly each time the paper was published. Regardless of how much I pleaded, Susie would not let me see the paper before everyone received one during seventh hour. Susie's dedication and pride in *Tom-Tom* made a lasting impression on me.

After class one day, Susie approached me, asking if I would like to write a story for *Tom-Tom*. I am still not sure what made me agree to try. Susie assured me that she would help me, but made it clear that she knew I could do a good job on my own. I had recently decided that I needed to start over-riding my fears of rejection and get involved in more school activities. So I pulled together all of my courage and accepted the assignment.

Susie continued to encourage me and bring me story assignments. I spent hours writing, rewriting, and editing each story I wrote. My family was forced to hear each one many times over as I asked for advice. In April, Susie made sure that I had an application for the staff and that I was planning to apply.

I spent hours preparing myself for rejection before the staff list was posted. I did not realize how completely unnecessary my worrying was until last year, however. After finals, some friends and I went out to lunch. At the restaurant I saw the former newspaper sponsor and said hello. She congratulated me on our final issue and for being selected as the Editor-in-Chief of *Tom-Tom*. Then she casually mentioned that she and Russell (the Editor-in-Chief my freshman year) had not only agreed that I should be on the staff, but that I could also eventually become the editor. I excused myself and rushed to the bathroom so that I could digest this overwhelming news by myself.

"Hey Jill—I'm counting on you to add some strength to *Tom-Tom*—next year looks like it may be rough, but I really think you'll do well—you've got what it takes to go the distance," wrote Susie in my yearbook. When there are problems on the staff now—and Susie was right about the rough year that followed—I think of her. Sometimes I get so frustrated with people that want to quit. But I never do. Susie made me love *Tom-Tom* more than anything else in the school. Even when I want to, I cannot turn away. I would disappoint myself.

Susie had (and still has, actually) a great influence on me. She showed me an ideal for the newspaper and for myself. Now I am aiming even higher than that ideal. Susie gave me confidence in myself at a time I needed it badly. I can see now that I already had the skills and drive, but that I needed a push. Susie gave me the push and I will never forget it. Now I owe it to her to give someone else the same push.

—JILL TROY

COMMENT: Jill's description of a friend and role model is a compliment, but most importantly it shows how she herself developed values. The essay is fine for the reader who is willing to follow the chronology of Jill's account.

*   *   *

Lately, a popular topic of conversation for Crossroads' seniors has been Life After High School. Most of us have plans to go to college, but few of us know what to expect once we get there. Our increasing anxiety is no secret to our advisor, who recently devoted two days of Senior English to the defining and discussion of the stereotype of the typical college student.

Our definition involved phrases like "obsessed with upward mobility," "not a risk-taker," and "super-conservative." We had painted quite a grim picture of our own generation—grim, and therefore not completely accurate. We figured that the word "conservative" was a neutral term with which to break the ice. One person thought it was an apt description because of the differences between our generation and a more radical group, college students of the 1960's. Another pointed out that our generation's return to traditionalism synonymously makes a return to conservatism.

I was thinking that this couldn't be true. Students of the sixties may have staged violent protests against Vietnam, but often it was because their greatest fear was that if they didn't end the war soon, they would be on the next planes flying into it. The issue on today's college campuses is divestiture of American investments in South Africa—our way of protesting gross human rights violations by economically affecting our target. To those who found us traditional, I pointed out that though we believe in marriage, we don't believe a married woman must end her career. To me, a combination of traditional values and liberal viewpoints seem to set the new generation of "conservatives" apart from past groups.

I think that the significance of being a young generation with a unique concept of itself is that we can successfully bring about constructive change.

Finally, we decided Crossroads' seniors of 1986 called itself "conservative" because we know how to bring about change by respecting authority and working through channels. When the senior class requested the right to drive off-campus during free periods, for example, a proposal outlining qualifications for drivers and passengers and including punishment for infractions was submitted to the Upper School Advisory Board. After refining the proposal and obtaining the necessary signatures, the measure passed. I concluded that being labelled "conservative" was not detrimental to us. Rather, it may be the very quality necessary to empower us with the ability to change negative situations.

These points seemed to clarify our generation's stereotype by dispelling the components "obsessed with upward mobility" and "not a risk-taker," along with the belief that "conservative" is synonymous with "traditional." It is clear we are concerned with social issues, not just social status, and we are willing to take risks to protect the rights of our fellow human beings. Though our values may be traditional, the viewpoints under which they lie are not. The "conservatism" of the generation to which these things contribute enables us to create constructive changes and corrects our once-negative stereotype to a positive one.

At the conclusion of our discussion, it dawned on me why I am so much happier here at Crossroads than I was at Smith High. The positive image created by my class, a good description of me as well as the group, could not have existed at my former school, where the boisterous atmosphere seemed nonconducive to original thinking. This realization served to strengthen my confidence in myself, my class, and the choices I am making for my future.

—RANDI S. CHERVITZ

COMMENT: Randi takes a big topic head on: How would she describe her generation? In doing so, she evaluates her classmates' views, and finally grounds the discussion in its relevance to herself. Thoughtful!

THE "PERSON YOU MOST ADMIRE" QUESTION

The following essays show several ways the students have answered the question, "Who is the person you most admire?" This question and its variants are frequent ones on admission forms. It generally elicits an interesting variety of responses.

A student at Harvard College, Susan Kopman, chooses to write about Carl Sagan, in particular his sense of intellectual curiosity and enthusiasm. Teresa Cotton from St. Louis Public School's Metro High, now at Wellesley College, discusses how Dr. Martin Luther King's many admirable qualities have had a profound effect upon her. Laura Geiser from Nerinx Hall High in Webster Groves, now at St. Louis University, tells us of the excitement of a freshman composition class and the exemplary teacher who taught her to look at things from a new perspective. Last, Emily Blumenfeld of Trinity College in Connecticut, describes her visit to an Indian reservation and her talks with a tribal medicine man.

* * *

Any man who would attempt to write a book "about the exploration of the universe and ourselves" must be a lover of knowledge and believer in the Socratic philosophy that men should lead examined lives. While some may criticize Carl Sagan for tackling too many branches of science, from astronomy to neurobiology, I consider this breadth of interests indicative of an admirable passion for learning. His passion is paralleled by a genuine joy in his work. And I find his enthusiasm inspiring.

After watching the series "Cosmos" for a second time, I discovered *The Dragons of Eden* one day while looking through my sister's bookcase. I found Dr. Sagan's "speculations on the nature and evolution of human intelligence" entertaining and provocative, and reading this book has helped me focus my hopes to study both biology and psychology at Harvard. While I cannot predict what specific path I will follow in my studies, the prospect of analyzing human behavior scientifically intrigues me. I believe that this interest has been inspired greatly by Dr. Sagan's own fascination with the subject; his enthusiasm for learning, whether it be in the study of the mind or the Milky Way, is contagious.

In "Cosmos" and in his narration of books and articles, Carl Sagan seems as full of questions as the five year old friend and neighbor for whom I babysit and as rational as even my seventh grade grammar instructor. His persona exudes both an educated skepticism and a wonderfully childlike curiosity and awe. A skeptical curiosity, integral to the process of learning, is a gift available to all of us. Carl Sagan is not extraordinary in retaining this innate human characteristic, but he is exemplary in revealing it in his work and striving to stimulate it in others. Analyzing, doubting, and wondering with enthusiasm, he manifests the keys to leading a life well examined.

Dr. Sagan writes in his introduction to *Broca's Brain* that "understanding is a kind of ecstasy." In this book "about the exploration of the universe and ourselves," he examines topics varying from Einstein's Theory of Relativity to "Clever Hans, the Mathematical Horse" with objectivity and respect. With an open mind and careful scrutiny, he asserts the probable and dismisses the unlikely only after close examination. Throughout these inquiries, as in his other works, his tone and humor indicate the enjoyment he finds in exercising his intellect.

Ralph Waldo Emerson wrote that "Men love to wonder, and that is the seed of science." Carl Sagan has not only such a curiosity and the skepticism crucial to rational thinking but also that quality which Emerson said "Nothing great was ever achieved without"—enthusiasm.

—SUSAN G. KOPMAN

COMMENT: Susan talks about Sagan, but she talks about herself too in this essay that focuses on one aspect of Sagan's significance. Susan narrowed the topic so that her complex ideas could appear. The complexity and specificity of Susan's views are matched by stylistic excellences: precise word choice, varied and elegant sentence structures, competent use of quotations. The essay speaks well for Sagan—and for Susan.

* * *

In my opinion, Dr. Martin Luther King, Jr., was one of the greatest Americans who has ever lived. Dr. King was intelligent, determined and bold. He was both a leader and a peacemaker. He lived his life to benefit others. For these reasons I admire Dr. King; he had all the qualities which define a successful person to me.

Much can be learned from someone of this caliber. Possibly the greatest attribute I would like to attain from this great man is his optimism. In Dr. King's time, ideas of equality for minorities were indeed a part of a dream. Yet he never gave up hope. Though he was imprisoned, threatened, taunted and denied personal freedoms, he did not compromise his position. His actions were done with the knowledge that he would probably not live to see his dream realized.

Altruism is another quality which I admire in Dr. King. He was a unique individual who found self satisfaction in doing for others. His efforts were not simply to better the lives of a select group, but so that all people would realize that discrimination in any form is evil. They also taught others that peace is a united effort.

In 1964, Dr. King was awarded the Nobel Peace Prize for his non-violent methods of obtaining equality. King felt that nonviolence was not only important but also necessary for achieving his goal.

Dr. Martin Luther King, Jr. is a positive role model and an inspiration for young people who are bombarded with critical decisions. It would not have been enough for me to work with this man: I would have liked to understand as he did. I'd like to know success as he defined it, for it is the same success that so many people such as myself seek.

Just as Dr. King had a dream for all people, I have a personal dream of my own: to be the very best that I can. In my academic endeavors, my relations with others and my self-esteem, I hope to excel. Where there is hope, there is possibility.

Dr. Martin Luther King, Jr., has passed into myth. Yet his memory lives on along with his dream in that so many people pattern their lives and ideals of peace after his. From this, I recognize the importance of not only having a dream but also working towards making that dream an actuality.

—TERESA COTTON

*   *   *

I met her my freshman year. She taught freshman composition. A class which I entered expecting a boring repeat of the eighth grade. It wasn't. Yes, there were the same participles, adjectives, and subjects, but somehow she made them fit together differently. When she taught us to write, the words found a meaning they never knew before. After her class, writing was no longer a problem because it had become something which I controlled. With her, writing was more than a challenge. With her, writing was fun.

The next time our paths crossed I was a senior. This time she was teaching literature. However, I'd been reading for years. I didn't really expect a challenge. Once again, I was wrong. With her help, I found a man who turned into a rather large bug, a cowardly lion hunter named Francis, and for whom the bell was tolling all along. I unearthed a Grecian urn and an out-of-the-way route to Byzantium. Next I discovered a confused prince of Denmark, and that I could read the dreaded Shakespeare. As a matter of fact, to my surprise (but not to hers) I realized that I liked him. I travelled through a doll's house and started paying attention to stage lighting. A few weeks ago I sat in on the funeral of a salesman, and then debated tragic heroism with my entire class. I found myself laughing at French plays written before our nation was born, much less me. Just the other day I contrasted an aged English king to a man fit for all seasons.

She doesn't know it, and probably never will, but she has literally changed my life. I look at things differently than I did before I met her. Somewhere down the line, when I've forgotten how to bisect a triangle, I know that I'll remember her.

—LAURA GEISER

COMMENT: Laura's tribute to her freshman comp teacher is only partly in what she says about her. It is also in Laura's documentation of the things the teacher taught her. This documentation reflects well on Laura and the teacher.

*   *   *

When I first heard about Tim Abel, the medicine man, I had many visions of his appearance and the way his presence would affect me. I had always envisioned men of such high honor as being extremely impressive and creating a strong aura of greatness. People who knew him piqued my curiosity but did not

confirm much. He was a man, or legend, whose reputation pre-
ceded him.

However, when I first caught a glimpse of Grandfather Abel
through the passenger window of his pick-up I was quite disappointed. Slowly climbing down from the cab, he stood to his
full height, only about 5'8". He was wearing Wrangler jeans, a
red and white checked shirt, and tennis shoes which looked as
if they had come from K-Mart. On his head was a cheap straw
cowboy hat with a feather hat band. Then, taking a closer
look, I noticed his jewelry and his face. On his wrist he wore a
magnificent silver and turquoise watchband that had incredible
handwork and the largest stones I have ever seen. His belt
buckle was of comparable worth and just as beautiful. His face
matched his jewelry. Old and wrinkled, it looked as if it had
been carved from leather, leather that was hard and cracking
from exposure to the elements, much like fine turquoise looks.
His features were sharply defined and his grey eyes peered
brightly out of the leathery visage. A line across his face turned
up at the edges and formed a smile which radiated a feeling of
contentment and a sense of knowledge. As he let his smile
broaden, I caught a glimpse of his rotten teeth. They were rotten from age and probably lack of care.

As time passed, his personality was still unclear. His features
were well defined, but his insides were of a different world.
This world was ancient. He tried to help me understand and to
pass his stories and the history of his people on to me, hoping
that I would not let his thoughts and dreams die. His wish
seemed to be that through these stories a part of him could live
on forever.

Speaking only Navajo, he used a translator, his daughter.
However, she was not always necessary. We sat in silence
around a fire. In that silence he let me know that he had a purpose, a reason for being there. Looking in his eyes, I could see
years of knowledge and of faith in his work. He could cure people with gifts from the earth and prayers to God. He had saved
many lives, and healed so many souls.

I look around the reservation and saw the way he lived, but he was happy. His life was what he wanted it to be. He helped others and was their friend. He held on to the past traditions but also looked to the future with bright hope.

As we finished dinner, he began to chant. He made me drink herbs and then sprinkled me with the liquid. He danced and walked around the fire and asked me to drink again. His daughter told me he was blessing me. He was taking me into his heart and loving me as one of his own.

After finishing the ceremony, the old man climbed into his truck and drove away. A strange feeling came over me; I felt tired and drained. It was as if Grandfather had left part of his spirit behind especially for me. Even as I think of him now, I feel his presence, not the presence of a man, but the presence of his soul.

—EMILY BLUMENFELD

COMMENT: An unusual subject keeps the reader's interest. And the subject allows Emily to show the excellence of her specific observations, and her ability to record description.

THE "PERSON YOU WOULD MOST LIKE TO SPEND A DAY WITH" QUESTION

Nicole Neuefeind and Jill Troy are both from the same class at University City High School and both now attend Stanford University. Nicole selects Christopher Columbus while Jill chooses singer Harry Chapin. A student from the Bartlesville, Oklahoma, schools, Craig May, also current at Stanford, selects Socrates.

* * *

I would like to spend a day with Christopher Columbus, specifically, the day in 1492 when he convinced Ferdinand and Isabella of Spain to sponsor his voyage to India by a daring new route—westward. I would ask him how, after having his idea rejected by the English, French, and Portugese courts, he found the courage to ask yet another monarch to support him. His faith in the scientific theory that the earth was round, which was accepted only by the intellectual elite, was admirable. Despite the fact that most people still adhered to the belief that the earth was flat and that ships would fall off the edge if they sailed too far in any direction, Columbus trusted the scientific evidence that proved the contrary. I would like to hear what Columbus said to the King and Queen of Spain to convince them that this plan would be profitable for them, when they knew that he had been turned down by three other monarchs. Any amount of money, supplies, or men with which they provided him could potentially be a total loss. In the eyes of the public, Columbus was risking his life, in addition to a number of ships and other lives, to attempt a voyage of doubtful success westward to India. I would like to get to know him and find the source of his great motivation.

—NICOLE NEUEFEIND

194

COMMENT: The essay shows that Nicole knows a lot about Columbus, and has thought about him. The reader still wonders—why *this* person as the choice for the essay?

* * *

I would like to spend a day with the late folk singer and songwriter Harry Chapin, singing and discussing love and life. That must sound very "flower child"-like, but that may be an accurate term to describe me. His songs ask questions and address human issues that interest me.

We could talk about his song, "Why Do Little Girls," and the roles society conditions children—even now—to fill. "Little girls were told to reach the shelves while little boys reached for the stars," he sings. This line brings endless questions to my mind. How can you break with tradition? How did traditional roles develop? How do you fight ideas? What are the values of the traditional family roles? Life and music are not full of only injustice and pain, though, so we could sing "The Circle" and smile until we cried. Harry's song "Seventeen" pulls together my love for standing up for what I believe and my faith in people. His music assures me that I am not alone. Harry Chapin represents peace and concern for mankind to me more than anyone else. Spending a day with Harry Chapin would be an experience I would treasure.

—JILL TROY

COMMENT: The choice of Chapin, Jill says, reflects something about the writer. She makes clear why she chose this folk singer for her subject.

* * *

The person I would most like to spend a day with is the Greek philospher Socrates. This may sound a bit trite, but I am truly fascinated by the man and his thinking. His philosophical ideas still endure today, 2500 years after his death. Not only was he a great thinker, Socrates was also a great teacher. The idea of spending a day with one of the greatest thinkers and teachers of all time is very appealing. I would spend the day like many of Socrates's pupils did; talking with the great man about life, death, truth, and reality. I can picture something straight out of Plato's dialogues, where Socrates, Plato, and myself do nothing but talk all day. Ideally, by the end of the day I would be completely "enlightened." This probably would not happen, though. What would happen if Socrates would ask me questions that I could not answer because I had never thought about them before? I would be confused and perplexed, and, before I knew it, the day would be over and my head would hurt. Maybe I would have learned nothing, but I doubt it. More than likely, I would have learned a little about Socrates, a little about "truth," and a lot about myself. As long as we went some place nice for lunch, it would be a perfect day.

—CRAIG MAY

COMMENT: This starts out as a competent, fairly undistinguished essay. But the last line shows us that Craig has a sense of humor, and does not take himself too seriously. The reader smiles along with Craig.

THE "DESCRIBE YOURSELF WITH ONLY ONE ADJECTIVE" QUESTION

Duke's Todd Wilcox responds to this question by stressing his willingness to accept responsibility.

Describing a person with one adjective is tantamount to judging the quality of a box of chocolates on one chocolate-almond froica. However, in answering this question, I have decided that the word "responsible" is the one word that most people would use to describe me.

In reviewing my life, the one quality I see running through everything I've done is my willingness to accept responsibility. Inherent in my psychological character-sketch is a feeling that enjoyment varies directly with responsibility. Consequently, I firmly believe that the successes I have had in life result from attempting to invest responsible, quality time in all aspects of my life. In addition, I feel that my responsibility also takes the form of accepting rewards as well as being accountable for failures. As a result, I find myself concentrating not merely on completion of a project, but completion of that project in a form in which I feel satisfied.

When the above is boiled down to a parable, a phrase something like "Responsibility Begets Quality" appears. Essentially, I have based a tremendous amount of what I have accomplished in my life on such a "simple" maxim. My academic work, extracurricular activities, church and community involvement, and personal lifestyle have all benefited from this philosophy. Hopefully, such a personal code will enable me to achieve the goals I have set for the future.

—TODD WILCOX

COMMENT: Todd opens with a mouth-watering analogy. The rest of the essay is solid and intelligent, but would be more impressive if he had given us specifics.

THE QUESTION IN WHICH YOU ARE ASKED TO ESTABLISHED A NEW PUBLIC HOLIDAY

Stanford's Nicole Neuefeind answers this question by citing a desire to commemorate the Mars landing of the Viking spacecraft, not only for its scientific achievements, but also for its universal appeal. Jill Troy, also of Stanford, wishes to create a holiday to celebrate peace and freedom. A third student from Stanford, Craig May, proposes to honor veterans of the war in Vietnam with a special holiday, citing this recognition as long overdue.

* * *

Given the authority, I would establish a holiday on July 20th to commemorate the touchdown of the two Viking landers on Mars on that date in 1976. The landing, which was the first actual contact of any earth space vehicle with another planet, represents the first step of humanity towards exploring other worlds. Though the ships were unmanned and no actual human contact with the Martian surface occurred, people were able to study Mars' surface and analyze its soil and atmosphere with the help of programmable machines that transmitted data. The landing of the Vikings on Mars is more important than the first step of man on the moon, because the moon is merely a satellite of the earth, not another planet with an orbit around the sun, like earth's. Though people now know that Mars' atmosphere is not sufficient to support life, the possibility did exist, whereas on the moon, life is not possible because it simply has no atmosphere. In addition, a holiday commemorating a scientific achievement is secular and could be celebrated by people of all religions. Because the landing on other planets is useful only for pure scientific research, the holiday would also be non-military and could be celebrated internationally.

—NICOLE NEUEFEIND

*   *   *

I would establish a holiday to commemorate peace and freedom if I could. I believe that too many of our present holidays are war-related. We yearly honor the people who fought for our country and vow not to forget their sacrifices. We do forget, however. We again become involved in war and more people die. We honor military figures who orchestrated great massacres of our "enemies." We do not honor the peace makers, however. We do not set aside days just to appreciate freedom and peace.

I think that the American idea of freedom is unfortunately misguided. The great American example of freedom is generally thought to be gaining our independence from Great Britain. Not all Americans were free after the Revolutionary War, however. Black Americans did not begin to gain their freedom for more than eighty years after the United States gained its freedom. My proposed holiday would, hopefully, bring more attention to peace and encourage us to realize the importance of our freedom.

—JILL TROY

*   *   *

With the tremendous number of national holidays, it is difficult to choose an event that has not already been commemorated. Yet, one group of people deserves a national holiday more than any other; the Vietnam Veterans. I realize we already have a Veterans' Day, but it does not seem appropriate for Vietnam Veterans. Veterans' Day is for veterans from the wars that we won. The United States does not like losers. As a nation, we did not even totally approve of the war in Vietnam. But, like it or not, brave men risked and gave their lives there when their country asked them to do so. They deserved to be honored, instead they were scorned. I may be completely naive about the atrocities of the war, but I believe that a man who does his duty for his country should be honored by his country. Are we so ungrateful that we scorn men who were brave enough to serve their country? Recently, there has been a change in the way the United States views the war in Vietnam. A memorial has finally been built in Washington, D.C., and people are becoming more sympathetic towards the war. I cannot understand why it has taken so long, but it is about time we give the Vietnam Vet the honor that was and is his due.

—CRAIG MAY

QUESTIONS TO WHICH STUDENTS RESPOND BY DISCUSSING SPECIFIC COLLEGES AND ACADEMIC PROGRAMS

Sara McCormick writes to the University of Michigan and stresses her involvement in high school activities and her enthusiasm for spending four years at Ann Arbor. Jason Barton of John Burroughs School, now at Lawrence University, tells why he wants to attend a particular school. A Yale student answers the question, "Describe the kind of college experience you are looking for as it relates to your expectations." Todd Wilcox of Duke describes the personal insights he gained at a summer program called Frontiers of Science sponsored by the University of Northern Colorado. The Merit Scholarship Program requests a brief essay of its applicants. Aaron DiAntonio writes of his future goals and tells of some of his interests. Aaron received the scholarship and is currently at Harvard College. Finally, Connie Willey, applying from Meramec Junior College, tells of her desire to participate in government and her commitment to work on behalf of others. Connie's essay was for a Truman Foundation Scholarship which she received. She is currently studying at Washington University.

*   *   *

Long autumns and chilling winters appeal to the student in me. Crossing a snowy quadrangle with a backpack slung over one shrugged shoulder brings to mind the possible life at the University of Michigan. Visiting the Ann Arbor campus this summer, I could have been easily misled by the pleasant breeze and the full trees and green lawns. I know that the school year brings a completely different scene however. Clayton, Missouri, a suburb of St. Louis, has likewise suffered the midwest curse of deceivingly warm summers slipping into bitter, snowy winters. Storm windows go up and are bolted for the season, and I think about how I will not venture outside until the first thaw. It is cold, obvious in the ice crystalled to the window. Principle enters my thoughtfulness: somebody will soon step into my undisturbed scene. I am going to enjoy it. Throwing on a coat and tying a scarf hastily, I abandon my reflection on the meaning of anything and pounce on the thrill of nature. I expect that I won't be the first to trudge through the snow of a university campus. I will cross the Quad with a backpack slung on my shrugged shoulder in the pace of the other boots which have left snowy impressions before me.

Winter is felt in the chilly changing air of Clayton. We wonder if we will have snow for Christmas. I am no exception, but I go one step further to wonder what my seasons next year will be. I am leaving my home and my secure, familiar community. I am comfortable. Clayton has been very good to me. I have had a job for two years and accepted the responsibility of opening and closing a restaurant as a night manager. During several summers I have worked as a camp counselor. I watch the children for whom I babysit grow from infancy to grade school. My teachers have honored me with initiation to the National Honor Society as a junior, as well as with their friendships. My friendships with other students and faculty have developed through many activities: I am Layout Editor for our school yearbook; I play varsity field hockey every year and I run track in the spring; I play Saturday basketball, which is a civic-sponsored athletic program; I sing and dance in our Broadway shows; I am involved in our Student Government and have served as an elected officer; and I participate in our Model U.N. program. My family has also been very important to me; they support and encourage me, while giving me a strong sense of independence and the opportunity to make decisions. I will have many friends and experiences to remember. The people here have given me a great deal:

experience, friendship, and worthy example. Clayton has given me confidence and so much more.

Now I am presenting myself as a prospective student to the University of Michigan. I have had many valuable experiences, and I know that the next four years will bring many more that will be very different. These next years will be very important to my character development, as well as to my academic future. I feel that the University of Michigan is the kind of school for which I am looking. I have enjoyed the academic emphasis of Clayton High School and my course choices have been varied. Math, languages, English, and history have been of special interest for me and I appreciate the high academic rankings of the University of Michigan in Ann Arbor in so many areas. Currently my brother, Michael, is a second year law student there, and his wife is in the graduate journalism program. Their enthusiasm for your university reinforces my own. If accepted, I hope that I can contribute to your school and give something of myself to it through my involvement, enthusiasm, and academic application; the possibilities are exciting.

I hope that we do have snow for this Christmas and for next year too. The snow may be here, but I know that the circumstances will be very different, as the Michigan snow that doesn't fall in Clayton.

—Sara McCormick

COMMENT: Sara provides a poetic frame for a list of her activities. If the list included were displayed elsewhere on the application, this essay would be repetitive. But if it was not, she has sugar-coated the pill nicely.

*   *   *

I first became interested in Generic College through Sharon Smith, who is both a friend and a neighbor, currently a senior at Generic and an alumnae of John Burroughs. This summer when weighing my college options, I asked her if she would be willing to come over and talk to me about Generic. She agreed enthusiastically and bored the daylights out of me. "Intensity, oh the intensity," she exclaimed. "It's so intense and I love it and I know you will too." She then topped this off by explaining about the vegetarian house where she lived; so thorough was her explanation that it seemed to me as if the whole campus went around eating tofu pizza. After hearing her talk about Generic, I began to think that it was not exactly the place that I had in mind: too farout, too intense, and too vegetarian.

Even though I was almost completely turned off, both my college advisor and my mother suggested that we go ahead and see the campus anyway, so I arranged a tour and interview this summer. The campus was nice, my interviewer especially so, but without classes in session, I couldn't get a feel for the real Generic, I decided to return for a fall visit. I came back convinced that I wanted Generic.

The three classes that I attended, one in freshman drama and two in reading fiction, excited my senses. The theatre class was reading a Chekhov play, and it seemed that the students were living their roles instead of merely reading them. The professor urged them on, and every student that read did so as if he or she were trying out for a Broadway show. Their intensity and their incredible amount of enthusiasm were infectious. In one of the English classes the students were discussing the central plot of *Wuthering Heights*. But their discussion transcended the arguments that were brought up in my high school discussions. Instead of simple generalities, they spoke of complex characterizations. Essentially they discussed the book on a level totally foreign to me—a level that was both new and intriguing.

I soon found even more that I liked about Generic. Stopping in Smith Hall, which provided me with a welcome relief from the steady downpour, on my way to the disco on a Friday

night; listening as Sean, my roommate, and some friends sin-
glehandedly composed a song for guitar and keyboard in less
than fifteen minutes—it was all of these things combined,
everything about Generic, that electrified me, scintillated me,
and most of all made up my mind that this was the place for
me.

Eventually, through my friend's invitation, I got to the
vegetarian house on my last night on campus, on the night that
they just so happened to be serving tofu pizza. My original
qualms still remained, but I went ahead and took a bite. And
guess what—I loved it!

—JASON BARTON

COMMENT: No doubt about it: Jason would convince
the reader that he had really thought about the virtues of
Generic. The tofu pizza at the end might not be to
everyone's taste, but the ending of the essay would be.

* * *

In this era of preprofessionalism, it is not chic to be idealistic about one's education, for idealism is often equated with
impracticality. I am idealistic, but not impractical. My interests
are primarily in those subjects that are not direct links to
preparation for prestigious careers, nor are they integral to pre-
anything programs. Generic University, with its Core Curriculum and consistent emphasis on a strong liberal arts program is
an obvious choice for a college.

Two of my favorite classes this year are A.P. French and
A.P. American History. In French, we studied Sartre's defini-
tive existential work, *Huis Clos*. In history, we are examining
the sociological effects of transcendentalism. I am planning to
continue this type of abstract study when I get to university.

To me, discussing existentialism in a foreign language is, in
many ways, more practical than taking more ostensibly useful

courses. Such courses may prep me for pre-med or law programs that will in turn prep me for graduate school, which will, in its turn, teach me all that I need to share in the American Dream, so that at 35 I can have a lovely house with a station wagon and 2.2 kids and summers on Hilton Head. Yet I contend that by learning to reason, I will eventually be able to convert my knowledge of the abstract and "impractical" matters into concrete skills that will allow me to be just as productive and useful as the realist. I am considering careers in journalism and sociology, both of which require a strong liberal arts education.

Perhaps I am an anachronism, more like a classical Greek scholar or a student during the Eisenhower years than a member of the job-conscious 1980s. It is all too easy to join the current "practical" education trend. I am prepared to take the risk of learning for learning's sake.

—ANONYMOUS

*   *   *

During the summer of my junior year, I had the opportunity to attend the Frontiers of Science Institute at the university of Northern Colorado. Founded in 1958, the program is an effort by University professors to expose science-oriented students to advanced concepts in science and math. Annually, thirty-two students are given scholarships by private industry to attend the eight-week study program. This Institute provided me with one of my most challenging intellectual experiences and, at the same time, provided me with a valuable opportunity to grow emotionally.

The academic life at Frontiers was divided into four segments—Organic Chemistry, Biology, Computer Science (FORTRAN), and Energy Science. During the week, I attended classroom sessions from 7:00 A.M. to 12:00 P.M., and in the afternoons, I spent a majority of my time in the labs conducting experiments or in the library doing additional research. On several of the weekends, the group took field trips to science-related locations, both in Colorado and in Wyoming. During the eight weeks, we visited the Martin Marietta Aerospace assembly plant, a national seed laboratory, the Johns Manville Research and Development Laboratories, several solar energy research houses, the Climax Molybdenum Analytical Laboratories, and the Eastman Kodak manufacturing plant. At each of these locations, as well as many others not mentioned, I saw the practical applications of the science I had been learning in the classrooms.

In addition to the general classwork, every student was required to pursue an independent research project. Through this project, I discovered not only how to ask pertinent questions, but also how to accomplish an in-depth research project successfully. My topic for the project was "The Pharmacological Effects of Supercooling Erythrocytes in a Dimethyl Sulfoxide Solution." Essentially, I investigated the possibilities of long-term storage of blood samples in a cryogenic atmosphere. Though my research does not qualify me for a Nobel Prize, it did teach me the importance of persistence, believing my observed data, and managing my time effectively. As a result, I believe that I am better prepared to enter a science program on the college level.

While Frontiers served as an intellectual stimulator, the personal benefits derived from such a program were priceless. For eight weeks, I lived in a college dorm with a close-knit group of thirty-two, thus requiring that I learn how to deal with the varied interests and the different lifestyles of the other students. I am thankful for my experiences at Frontiers of Science, and through my experience there, I feel that I have developed a deeper insight into my own life. I shared many magic moments with this group, and have developed friendships I will cherish for a lifetime. As a result of my time at Frontiers, I believe that as I attend college next year, I will have a better idea of what to expect of myself, both intellectually and emotionally.

—TODD WILCOX

COMMENT: A competent retelling of the program at Frontiers of Science Institute, informative for the reader unfamiliar with it. Todd makes assertions about its personal benefit to him, and convinces us the experience was an important one.

* * *

Sartre postulated that "Life has a meaning if we choose to give it one." While this concept may seem dated by contemporary standards, it embodies a philosophy to which I attempt to adhere. Science, with its inherent intricacies, mysteries, and exactitudes, is my chosen vehicle for achieving this goal. This past summer I was employed as a technician in the hematology department of the Washington University Medical School. I investigated sugar pool levels in divergent strains of cancerous tumor cells. While I most certainly did not discover a cure for cancer, I did, however, acquire an intense interest in scientific investigation. I anticipate working as a research biochemist and hope to contribute to an increased understanding of the cellular processes. While science is my primary interest, it is by no means my only interest. I have participated in theater throughout my high school career, including three lead roles in serious dramas. The musical comedy I authored was selected for production this year. As coordinator of our local Modern United Nations chapter, I have learned a great deal about international issues and foreign cultures. I avidly collect political memorabilia, an avocation that has piqued my interest in a political process in which I will soon be an active participant. It is my hope that these interests and aspirations will remain a part of what gives my life meaning as I face the pleasures and challenges of the future.

—AARON DIANTONIO

*   *   *

My long term goal is to participate in government either as an elected official or representative of an interest group which focuses on issues affecting women. If I am unable to attend law school, which is my first choice for post-graduate work, I would obtain a Master's degree which would allow me to teach. Additionally, I hope to find a format which will allow me to continue addressing public policy issues through writing.

My undergraduate degree is designed to enhance my writing and speaking skills. Hopefully this will assist me in efforts to communicate more effectively with the public. Furthermore, I plan to minor in political science or history in an attempt to better understand our governmental process and the events which have lead us to present day policy.

At the University of Missouri-St. Louis I plan to pursue, in addition to the above, a Certificate in Women's Studies. It is my belief a career in law or teaching will enable me to be more successful in facilitating change within our society which will allow women and other minorities to achieve equality.

As a divorced mother for many years I became acutely aware of the inequality, discrimination and barriers confronting women in our society. While we as a nation purport to hold children and families in high esteem, my experience was quite the opposite when faced with obtaining housing and child care as a single parent. While many Americans may condemn the welfare mother for staying home and the working mother for leaving her children, the single mother has no other choices.

The academic experience which awakened and nurtured my political consciousness was a political science course I took in the fall of 1984. During this time I became aware of the mechanisms which control our government and make change possible in our democracy. During the past year I have realized even more how fragile the rights of women and other minorities are and how easily these rights, which we "take for granted," can be lost.

Since my life circumstances have changed and I no longer need to be primarily concerned with "just surviving," I feel an obligation and commitment to work on behalf of those people who through ignorance, poverty, or circumstances beyond their control, are unable to speak out. I know someone was fighting for my rights when I was unable to. I owe a debt.

—CONNIE WILLEY

QUESTIONS RELATED TO READING

This group of essays deals with variants of the questions concerning books that have had an effect on the applicant. Megan Ferry from Mt. Holyoke College couches her observations regarding *The Catcher in the Rye* in a dramatic dialogue. A scholarship applicant discusses reading preferences and then focuses upon Voltaire's *Candide*. Debbie Feldacker of the University of Chicago writes about Elie Wiesel's *Night*. Nicole Fitchner of Harvard relates her own experiences to those of Joyce's *A Portrait of an Artist as a Young Man*.

* * *

Is my hunting hat not on straight? Good, that's better. Here is the world famous reporter, Megan M. Ferry on special assignment to New England to stalk the true J.D. Salinger, author of *The Catcher in the Rye*. What an exciting report this is going to be.

And here he comes now. He's walking toward me down the path. Wait, what should I say? He's walking slowly, in-between the shadows, head bent in self-pitying placid contemplative thought. I want to just run up to him and smother him with questions. But then again, I'd probably scare him away.

But shouldn't a sensitive reader be entitled to talk to the sensitive writer? I should ask him just that. Isn't his writing his own mask shining through? I mean to say, one always hides one's insecurities with masks. Holden Caulfield's was trying to act older, but he still had to adjust it as it went askew. But sometimes the mask has a few flaws in it. Like when Holden met the mother on the train, and how he told her he had a brain tumor. Wasn't it obvious he was lying?

Hey, I wonder how much of a Holden, J.D. Salinger actually is. What kind of mask does he live behind? How would he

211

answer me? Of course, he's very elusive, so I'd have to be rather coy with the phrasing of my questions. I shouldn't "lay it on too thick," so to speak. I think J.D. Salinger's mask must be his reclusiveness and writing. But isn't that the ill-fate of all writers that the written work is oneself exposed? I'd ask him that. Oh no, maybe I wouldn't. How would I phrase it? I wouldn't want him to think I'm naive or something. It should all be worded properly. Should I block his path and introduce myself to him? Or maybe, should I pretend I'm lost and just as soon as he gives me directions, should I start to question him?

No, no wait. Maybe it would be even better if the first question had nothing to do with him at all. For instance, the recipe for baked lasagna? No, I'd have to save that one for our second chance encounter.

I know, I'll ask him if he's happy. It's just like Holden's situation. I could feel so happy and laugh with Holden, but at the same time I felt sad and could cry for him. I'd love to tell him everything's all right and that I wouldn't try to tear his mask down. That sounds good. I'll put it a bit nonchalantly.

Okay, everything's set. I'm gonna do it. Wait, one more deep breath, fix the hat; I don't want to blow it in the first few seconds. This could be the beginning of a whole new career for me. Okay, now! . . . Oh, no, he's gone. He's simply disappeared. Maybe he went off to the left? No. Great, I've scared him off. I bet I thought too loud.

—MEGAN FERRY

COMMENT: The topic is familiar, but Megan gives it a fresh treatment, making appealing reading. Her pseudo-journalistic account of the proposed interview with J.D. Salinger shows originality and humor. The shape her essay takes shows creativity—and knowledge of her subject.

*   *   *

Having eclectic taste concerning literature, I have read works covering a broad spectrum from the ponderous to the frivolous. My most recent book was Jonathan Schell's *The Fate of the Earth*, which tied in quite nicely with *Disturbing the Universe*, by Freeman Dyson. Over the summer I greatly enjoyed *Lucy*, by Donald Johanson and Maitland Edey, and *The Real War*, by Richard Nixon. I read such popular works as John Irving's *The World According to Garp* and quite a few of Kurt Vonnegut's books, including my favorite, *Slapstick*. I also was impressed by James Clavell's *King Rat* and Michener's *The Source*. The most poignantly humorous book I read this last year, and possibly ever, was John Kennedy Toole's *A Confederacy of Dunces*. Further reading included several books by Ken Follett, the author of *The Eye of the Needle*. Periodicals I enjoy regularly are *Newsweek* and *U.S. News and World Report*. Yet of all the books I have read, the one that left the greatest impression was *Candide* by Voltaire, a work I read as background to my modern European history course. I was intrigued by both the work and its author, and therefore I am choosing it as the subject for this critical evaluation.

Voltaire used his writings and political influence to fight against arbitrary absolutism and religious fanaticism. He took a great interest in the philosophies of Pope and Leibnitz, who both were optimists. This interest was vitally important to *Candide*, which satirized his belief in optimism. The evil and suffering that Voltaire saw around him motivated him to write against Leibnitz's thesis that this is the best of all possible worlds. The horrible earthquake and resulting tidal wave that hit Lisbon in 1755 and killed over 30,000 people may have been the catalyst for the writing of *Candide*.

Candide is the essence of literary satire. It satirized the philosophies of the English writer Alexander Pope who believed that "whatever is, is right," and the German philosopher Leibnitz, who believed that God was good and so he created the best of all possible worlds. It is evident that Voltaire is satirizing optimism when the hero, Candide, defines optimism as "the folly of maintaining that everything is right, when it is wrong." Voltaire uses the character of Dr. Pangloss to represent Leibnitz's philosophy, and mercilessly attacks him with his rapier-like wit. Pangloss, who believes all things are for the best, contracts venereal disease and loses the tip of his nose, one eye, and one ear; endures a shipwreck and the earthquake of Lisbon; is hanged by the Inquisition, and is forced to row in the galleys. It is irony, verging on the ridiculous, that a man who believes this is the best of all possible worlds has suffered so dreadfully. Voltaire not only uses Candide's journey and the suffering he witnesses to ridicule the philosophies of Pope and Leibnitz, but also attacks various societal problems in Europe. As Will Durant said, *Candide* is "a telling satire of . . . religious abuses, monastic amours, class prejudice, political corruption, legal chicanery, judicial venality, the barbarity of the penal code, the injustice of slavery, and the destructiveness of war." During Candide's travels he visits Paraguay. "There the Jesuit Fathers possess all, and the people nothing; it is a masterpiece of reason and justice." Voltaire is obviously being sarcastic when he says this; he is denouncing the great disparity between the wealth of the religious men in South America and the poverty of the peasant class. Throughout the book religious men who should be celibate are not, including a Cordelier with venereal disease. Voltaire ridicules class consciousness by having Candide's mother choose to have an illegitimate son instead of marrying an honest gentleman because "he could only produce seventy-one armorial quarterings." Voltaire deals with the injustice of slavery when Candide meets a black slave who lost a leg and a hand in the sugar mill which, as the slave said, "is the price at which you eat sugar in Europe." Voltaire used satire to denounce societal problems in Europe, but the main object of Voltaire's savage wit was the optimistic philosophy of both Pope and Leibnitz.

Voltaire's thesis for *Candide* is summed up in his final quote, "Let us cultivate our garden." This seems to mean that we must each do our individual and immediate task. By using the word "cultivate," Voltaire is telling man to work. He believed in the work ethic, and that by working man could be kept "free from three of the greatest evils: tiresomeness, vice, and want." Throughout the book Voltaire attacks the belief in optimism, yet he does not take a totally pessimistic view of the world. Voltaire is saying that there is good and bad in the world, and that man must travel the narrow path between the two. Voltaire is postulating that we should change those things we can, but accept those things we cannot change, because no man can do more. Voltaire's thesis is that the world is "not all for the best," and hence, man is ultimately responsible for his own life, his own problems, his own "garden."

—ANONYMOUS

COMMENT: This one covers the bases: an annotated list of favorite books, and a more detailed view of *Candide*. Even a rushed admissions officer could skim this and be impressed. This is an essay that respects the overburdened reader.

*   *   *

Many books have been written about the Holocaust. However, none have the depth and poignancy that *Night*, by Elie Wiesel, possesses. *Night* is not only an account of the terrifying events of the Holocaust, the concentration camps, and the genocide, but also a description of the experiences of twelve-year-old Elie Wiesel who endures a numbness, even a separation of body and mind, as a result of his intense suffering.

In the first twenty pages, Elie Wiesel and the Jews in his area appear to be a highly pious group. Each day is spent in prayer and with family. When he and his family are evacuated and moved via cattle cars to Auschwitz, the suffering begins. Just days after Elie's arrival at the camp, Elie's father is clubbed a near-fatal blow. Elie watches him crawl on the ground but does not help him. His immobility is symbolic of the moral numbness that intense suffering and shock inflict. This condition of numbness, the mind's paralyzed state between learning and growing and deteriorating and dying, is prevalent throughout *Night*. The suffering Elie has already endured is consuming his mind.

By applying this concept, one sees how *Night* illustrates that an entire people can be exterminated. As one suffers intensely, reality is lost. The mind numbs and the victim becomes a corpse, unable to think or to act. This theme is well-known. In *Macbeth*, Macbeth kills King Duncan. After this event, he is so possessed and shocked by the fact he has committed such a crime that his mind numbs. He loses the ability to reason and brings the weapon used for the killing to his own chamber, unable to realize that he is identifying himself as the murderer. Though the situations are far from identical, the theme is the same. When a mind is possessed by suffering or shock, it numbs. Numbing is the mind's way of escaping reality. In the Holocaust, there was no other way of surviving with any sanity.

The latter stages of numbing involve the separation of mind from body. When Elie and his father are evacuated from the camp and forced to run forty-two miles, Elie survives by making his body a separate entity from his mind. His mind is becoming a corpse, completely numb from the horrors around him and his own physical pain. His body, suffering from hours of running and no food, is the only evidence that Elie is still human. His method allows him to ignore the death and suffering around him. The separation shows that a conscious mind rejects the suffering endured during the Holocaust. Like the schizophrenic who is traumatized to the point of changing personalities, the body is traumatized to the point of separation from the mind and soul.

The separation concept is intrinsic to the book. Elie is separated from his mother at the entrance to the camp. He is separated from his father at times. He is separated into a group allowed to eat, a group allowed to live. Even his age, thirteen, is representative of separation from childhood. At the same time, he is being further separated from his life of the past. One can see why Wiesel emphasizes the theme. The Holocaust in general was a separation, a separation of families, of Jews from humanity and of Nazi Germany from morality.

When the final liberation comes, Elie is able to look at himself in a mirror for the first time in three years. As he peers in, he realizes he does not recognize the face looking back at him. He is transformed. The suffering that he endured during the Holocaust, including the death of his father and his God, has changed Elie into a numb and empty corpse. This lack of self-recognition represents the degree of change a person undergoes when subjected to excessive suffering. Indeed, nobody who endured the Holocaust emerged the same person. I, too, as I read the autobiography, was deeply affected by the realization of the insanity in our world.

—DEBBIE FELDACKER

*   *   *

James Joyce's *A Portrait of the Artist as a Young Man* has exercised my mind to a greater extent than any book I have ever read. Probably the first and most obvious challenging aspect of this book is Joyce's language and style of writing. Upon starting to read the book, I struggled with both the vocabulary and the "stream of consciousness" poetic prose of the novel. At first, this random flow of ideas and feelings deterred me, but as I continued to read, I became progressively engrossed in the style, letting my mind become carried along in the stream of words. The second most challenging facet of the novel is the subject matter. It is difficult to picture late nineteenth century

Ireland as described by Joyce and to understand the major issues of the time. The religious and artistic ideas which trouble the young Stephan Dedalus are a drastic contrast to the problems encountered by Americans today. Yet, Joyce does pose numerous themes which can be understood universally. I find that these thought-provoking ideas have touched me in a personal way, occasionally affecting my behavior. Many of Stephan's painful experiences of childhood and growing up parallel my own recollections of homesickness and of making and losing friends. I find I especially relate to Stephan's life, as I am now a teenager myself. Like Stephan, I realize I am in a transitional period of my life, trying, almost blindly, to make important decisions about my future. Recently, religion and politics have confused me, and I have not been able to sort out and establish my views concerning them. These same issues baffle Stephan Dedalus, and as a result, he finally abandons both the Catholic church and the Irish political system to create his own "art" or individuality. I, too, am facing the question of what I will make of myself and my future and how I will create my own "art." I realize I need to conform to fit in with my peers, yet like Stephan, I know it is often more important to voice my opinions no matter how ludicrous they may seem. In effect, after reading *A Portrait of the Artist as a Young Man*, I have become concerned with who I am, and I am working harder to shape my own individuality.

—NICOLE FITCHNER

COMMENT: Nicole's essay on *Portrait of the Artist* shows that she not only read the book, but that she made it part of her life. No impersonal book review, this short account tells us about Joyce's book and Nicole's feelings.

THE "IMAGINE AN ALTERNATIVE OUT-COME TO AN HISTORICAL EVENT" QUES-TION

This question is designed to explore reasoning skills. Todd Wilcox of Duke University argues with the assumption of this question by focusing upon the inevitability inherent in the historical process in general.

*   *   *

Modern historical thought tends to preclude the possibility that the history of man is based on sporadic major events. Hence, to "choose an event in history and imagine an alternative outcome" is not possible, given the mosaic structure of human history.

Crane Brinton, in his *Anatomy of a Revolution*, deals with a certain inevitability inherent in all revolutionary movements, including religious, social, political, and economical. Essentially, Brinton argues that all revolutions begin with unrest in the intellectual classes of society, upon whence the politically moderate come to power. As the revolution proceeds, a reign of terror descends on society, with control in the hands of the deified heroes of the rebellion. Finally, a period of convalescence emerges, with characteristics of both the Old and New Regimes present in society. While this is quite a general review of Brinton, the universality of his formula is what is important. Whether the revolution be Chinese, French, Russian, American, or Iranian, history proves the formula true. Hence, to change an event within a revolution would obviously have little or no effect on the overall outcome, for the formula will tend to hold for all situations.

Outside of strictly "revolutionary" thought, the changing of one event in history would still have little effect on society as a whole. For example, Martin Luther is not responsible for the Reformation as we know it. He, in an innocent attempt to protest the selling of indulgences in Germany, served as the spark that ignited the societal gunpowder that had been building for years. Hence, even if Martin Luther had not been born, someone somewhere would still have provided that spark. Consequently, the intricate stockpiling of minor events to produce major events dictates that a change in history would not affect the outcome.

Evidence from many other historical events tends to support the atmosphere of "predestination" that is forwarded by Brinton. Hence, while the changing of one historical event may alter the route taken to the destination, it appears that the history of man truly does follow a pattern.

—TODD WILCOX

COMMENT: Todd intelligently questions the question. His answer suggests why the assumptions of the question are faulty. His ability to deal with the specific application question assures the reader that he is indeed responding to a particular school's request; his ability to work with a complicated idea testifies to his academic strengths.